# How to Make Money Performing in Schools

## The Definitive Guide to Developing, Marketing, and Presenting School Assembly Programs

**David Heflick**

**Silcox Productions, Orient, Washington**

# How to Make Money Performing in Schools

### The Definitive Guide to Developing, Marketing, and Presenting School Assembly Programs

### By David Heflick

Published by: Silcox Productions
P.O Box 1407
Orient WA 99160
(509) 684-8287

ISBN: 0-9638705-8-0 (soft cover)
LC Number: 96-92572

# Table of Contents

# Acknowledgments

Many individuals have provided assistance in bringing this project to fruition. I sincerely thank them all for their contributions. I wish to give special thanks to the following people who have either granted an interview for inclusion in the book, reviewed and evaluated manuscripts, or both: Newt Adams, Phyliss Barney, Lee Bash, Rob Caruano, Cory Crawford, Glenn Becker, Jim Eisenhardt, Venita Ellick, Micky Fisher, Brian Fox, Susan Lachman, Nancy Langan, Chris Lunn, Tim O'Brien, Dorothy Sasscer, Jana Stanfield, Larry Stein, Elaine Thatcher, Ellen Weinstein, Nan Westervelt.

Special thanks to Cynthia Tierney for countless hours of reading and proofing manuscripts, and to Roberta Greene for assistance in helping me comprehend the rules of grammar and punctuation and for editing the final manuscript.

Also, a special word of thanks to Bruce Brummond, who introduced me to the idea of performing in schools and provided guidance and encouragement when I was first getting started.

*To Cindy, whose gift for working with children
has had a profound effect on both my career and my life.*

# INTRODUCTION
## About This Book

A school assembly program should do more than entertain students, it should educate them as well. For the program to achieve its educational objective, the artists presenting the program must take an active role in engaging, involving, and managing the audience. The goal of this book is to equip performing artists with the necessary skills to design a top-quality program, effectively present it to young audiences, and earn significant income while doing so. Part One provides step-by-step instructions relevant to artists of all disciplines. Part Two contains interviews, program descriptions, and program theme ideas for each of the major discipline areas: music, theater, dance, and speaking.

Throughout the book I have included, where appropriate, examples, personal experiences, and insights from my ten years experience performing in schools. Whenever I refer to *my duo*, or *we*, the reference is to the *Dave & Cindy Duo,* which consists of myself and my partner in both music and marriage since 1981, Cynthia Tierney.

# Part One:
## Program Design, Marketing, and Presentation

# CHAPTER 1
# The School Market

The information in this chapter, based largely on interviews with school principals, will provide a working knowledge of the school market. Understanding what school administrators look for in assembly programs will lend direction and focus to the subsequent steps of program design, promotion, and presentation.

## Entertainment vs. education

*Since there are so many demands on our time, I can't afford to have just any Joe Blow in here...I'm looking for something that is going to have some educational value and, at the same time, be enjoyable for the kids.* - Cory Crawford, Principal, Fruitland ES, Puyallup WA

Most schools are looking for programs that are both entertaining and educational, with the emphasis on education. School administrators are under enormous pressure to account for the educational value of every minute of the school day. If students will be leaving their classrooms for an assembly program, the principal wants to know that the time will be well spent. With rare exception, principals are not interested in programs that get kids cheering and having a good time while learning nothing.

Principals use assembly programs for a variety of reasons.

9

Sometimes they are interested in spotlighting a particular art form. At other times, they look for programs that highlight the importance of a particular holiday, address a current social issue, inspire their students to become more responsible citizens, or enhance grade-level curriculum.

## Arts-education programs

*I try to bring in an opera group each year...a dance group...I try to use assemblies as a way to expose kids to various art forms.* - Newt Adams, Principal, Clarkmoor ES, Tacoma WA

In cases where the principal is seeking to focus on a particular art form, a performance alone may satisfy his requirements. More often though, he will look for a program that, in addition to exposing students to a performance, has a theme addressing the history of the art form, the various styles of the art form, or the technology and skills required for performing works or pieces.

In response to budget cuts in arts-education programs, some states have passed laws requiring schools to present a certain number of performances during the course of the year, providing students with at least some exposure to the arts. Principals in these states actively seek presentations of music, theater and dance in order to meet these requirements.

## Ethnic programs

Many principals are interested in promoting an appreciation for the ethnic diversity of the world, looking for programs about the history and culture of Native Americans, Asians, Africans, and other ethnic groups. Often principals seek to tie the educational content of these programs into classroom curriculum or present the program in conjunction with national observances.

## Programs with calendar connections

Principals often seek programs that will help their students

10

better understand holidays such as Veterans Day, Earth Day, Martin Luther King Jr. Day, or Memorial Day. Some schools are required by state law or district mandate to present such programs. Principals also like programs with themes that elaborate on the significance of special weeks or months in the year such as *Black History Month* or *Drug Abuse Prevention Week*, often booking artists who have a special program that uses music or theater as a medium to convey a message about the observance. In these situations, the art form itself is of secondary importance.

## Curriculum connections

*We're trying to do more integrated instruction, so we're interested in programs that tie different subject areas together: art, with things like social studies and science and literature.* - Tim O'Brien, Principal, Issaquah Valley ES, Issaquah WA

*Because assemblies are as expensive as they are, we usually try to stick with things where the educational theme is broad enough to address all the grade levels. But if a program also ties into the specific curriculum of one of our classes, that's an additional incentive.* - Venita Ellick, Principal, Gordon ES, Kingston WA

With a renewed emphasis on integrated instruction, programs that build bridges between subject areas or tie into the curriculum of a particular grade level while remaining general enough in scope to be of interest to all students are popular with principals.

For example, fourth-grade students are studying Washington State history. A folk-music ensemble with a presentation consisting of songs with roots in the state's history is booked to present a program. A general theme about folk music is developed in the program, providing an arts-education experience for all students. In addition, program content draws connections between the songs and the state's history, enhancing the Washington State history curriculum for the fourth-graders.

11

# Excerpts from interviews with principals

*I tend not to be favorable toward assemblies that really go to the extreme of getting kids excited...because sometimes they get so charged up you can't get them down again—with several hundred kids in the auditorium, that can be a very tricky thing to do. -* Newt Adams, Clarkmoor ES, Tacoma WA

*We like to bring in things like jugglers and unicyclists. Not so much so that they can thrill and entertain us, but so that the kids can see that while they may not be as skilled as the artists, they are capable of doing those things; it just requires time and effort. -* Cory Crawford, Fruitland ES, Puyallup WA

*We're interested in programs where the art form is used to develop a topic or content area we are currently studying or focusing on...*

*...My main concern is that the program be of sufficient interest and move at a quick enough pace that it holds the students' interest. It's surprising: it isn't necessarily the stuff with a lot of glitz that holds their attention...it's the involvement of the students and the pace of the presentation rather than pyrotechnics. -* Tim O'Brien, Issaquah Valley ES, Issaquah WA

*It's hard to find presentations on things like developing students' manners and character, morals and values (while avoiding the difficult or controversial issues), and friendship...If there was something like that available, I would love to have it in the fall as a kickoff to the school year. Also, there are not a lot of programs on substance abuse. -* Venita Ellick, Gordon ES, Kingston WA

*I've seen too many programs where the performers are not good teachers and they really don't know how to manage students. -* Jim Eisenhardt, Yelm Prairie ES, Yelm WA

*There may be times when we want to emphasize an art form, so we'll bring in an assembly to do that. But most often, we book programs based on the topic that's being developed, and the art form used to convey that message is secondary. -* Brian Fox, Karshner ES, Puyallup WA

## Study guides

*It is helpful to get study guides before a program; that way we can brief the kids on what they will see during the program. The kids will have a better understanding of the program theme, and they can participate more effectively.* - Tim O'Brien, Principal, Issaquah Valley ES, Issaquah WA

Most principals feel that study guides increase student retention of the educational content of a program. They stressed, however, that the study guides should be brief and well organized and that suggested activities should involve materials readily available in the classroom.

## Program length

*If you're going over half an hour, you're stretching it—you'd better be good.* - Jim Eisenhardt, Principal, Yelm Prairie ES, Yelm WA

*If your most important points are at the very end—beyond the thirty minute mark—the students won't retain it.* - Brian Fox, Principal, Karshner ES, Puyallup WA

Most principals feel that thirty minutes is the maximum length of time one can expect K-3 students to remain attentive; forty-five minutes is the consensus regarding fourth- through sixth-graders. One principal interviewed indicated that he felt many performers over-estimate these maximum lengths by an average of ten minutes.

## Wild or mild?

*I've seen shows where the performers hype the kids up—get kids standing up and screaming and hollering; going back to the classroom, the teachers just hate it, because the kids are out of control.* - Brian Fox, Principal, Karshner ES, Puyallup WA

*I like to see the kids having fun—to see them laughing and cheering, but I like to see the performer bring them back down so they are not sending them back to their classrooms just higher than a kite.* - Jim Eisenhardt, Principal, Yelm Prairie ES, Yelm WA

Many principals feel that enthusiasm is too often sought at the expense of audience control. Some don't like to see the kids get hyped up at all—they're trying to teach the kids *not* to behave that way unless the assembly is a pep rally or similar event. Those who believe that such behavior is not always inappropriate, feel that performers who get the audience cranked up should also have the skills to bring them back down quickly. They also feel that performers should not, under any circumstances, get the kids fired up right before the end of the program—that artists should end with something soothing, making for a smoother transition back to the classrooms.

## Budget realities

The artist's fee is an important factor as principals consider program offerings. Most principals, with rare exception, will not pay more than $700 for a show, no matter how great it is—not necessarily because the program isn't worth it, but because the expense will cut too deeply into the assembly budget. The average fee they expect to pay ranges from $300 to $600, depending on the nature of the ensemble and presentation.

## Summary

As far as principals are concerned, the ideal show will meet the following criteria:

- provide both educational value and entertainment value
- have a broad enough appeal to interest students of all grade levels
- be performed by artists who are more concerned with managing the audience than getting the kids visibly excited
- have correlating study guides
- be thirty to forty minutes in length
- not exceed $700 in cost.

Programs with the following educational themes are popular among principals:

- arts-education themes

- ethnic themes

- themes with connections to grade-level curriculum

- themes that relate to holidays and other calendar designations.

# CHAPTER 2
# Ingredients for a Successful Program

*You could come up with a template for presenters to use, but unless they've got that certain "something," it's not going to come off all that well.* - Cory Crawford, Principal, Fruitland ES, Puyallup WA

There is a certain magic at work in successful school assembly programs. In attempting to analyze these programs and the artists who present them, one invariably discovers that the total is greater than the sum of the parts. Any attempt to arrive at a formula or methodology upon which other programs might be designed is doomed to failure. However, there are a number of common characteristics shared by successful programs and the artists who present them.

## The performers

Successful children's performers exude a love for children and an enthusiasm for their work. They speak to the audience in a tone of kindness, their actions and words reflecting an awareness that they are not smarter or better than children, simply more experienced. The artists find joy in sharing their art form with children, approaching their work with a great deal of enthusiasm—enthusiasm that's visible, tangible, and infectious.

16

The artists' love and enthusiasm is reciprocated by the audience. Moments after the program has begun, the children are smiling, participating, and literally falling in love with the performers.

## Audience management techniques

*Successful artists constantly set things up in advance, letting the kids know how things are going to happen and what is expected of them. They encourage the kids when they follow instructions and give them a lot of feedback about how they are doing as an audience.* - Venita Ellick, Principal, Gordon ES, Kingston WA

All performers who are successful in schools utilize techniques to guide and control the audience. These techniques are always positive and gentle in nature and reflect an awareness that loss of audience control is much more likely due to unbridled enthusiasm resulting from what the performers are sharing, rather than a conspiracy to ruin the program. The artists set expectations for the audience, continually evaluate the children's conformance, and praise them when they meet the expectations. If the audience's behavior falls short of the mark, the artists remind students of the expectations and verbalize confidence that the children will succeed in meeting the expectations.

## Audience participation

Nearly all successful programs have some form of audience participation. At times, the entire audience participates through singing, physical movement, clapping rhythms, etc. At other times, individuals or small groups of students are selected to come forward and participate in performances, demonstrations, and other activities. Such involvement keeps the children engaged and moves the presentation from something to be observed to a participatory activity.

## Interesting narratives, dialogues, and skits

In many programs, the stated educational objective is largely accomplished through non-performance segments. These segments inform the audience about various aspects of the art form. While some performers somehow get away with a rather dry recitation of facts, most utilize stories, humor, skits, demonstrations, and other activities to bring the non-performance segments alive.

## Summary

While it is impossible to reduce the successful presentation of a program to a formula or methodology, there are certain elements that successful programs have in common:

- artists who love and respect children
- artists who have a genuine enthusiasm for their art
- artist who utilize techniques to manage the audience
- audience participation
- skits, demonstrations, and other activities.

# CHAPTER 3
# Developing a Program

While theater artists, puppeteers, storytellers, and other artists presenting works that essentially tell a story have the option of performing a single complete work as the content of their program, most school assembly programs are a montage of performance pieces, narration, dialogue, demonstrations, and activities. Through the process of developing a program, these segments are assembled in such a way that the theme of the program unfolds in a logical fashion.

The line between program development and program presentation (to be discussed in a later chapter) is a blurred one. For our purposes, we will make a distinction between the two as follows: program development includes all the planned parts of the program—the performance pieces, narrations, ways in which the audience will participate, demonstrations, and anything else constituting actual content of the program. Program presentation will be defined as the manner in which the artists perform, narrate, ask for participation, conduct demonstrations, etc. Think of it this way: program development is *what* you are planning to do, program presentation is *how* you are going to do it.

**Educational objective vs. program theme**

In the school setting, student learning results from the articu-

19

lation and subsequent accomplishment of educational objectives. An educational objective is a concise statement describing what the children will know or be able to do after they have listened to a lecture, completed an assignment, or taken part in any other activity designed to educate. Thus, the educational objective for an assembly program describes what the children will learn as they watch the program. For example, the following is the educational objective of a program consisting of a variety of American folk songs: Students will learn that American folk music is a vehicle of expression for a broad range of feelings and emotions, often stemming from specific events and eras in the history of our nation.

A program theme describes the program content through which the educational objective will be accomplished. For example, the theme of the program in the example above might be stated as follows: A historical overview of American folk music and its role as a vehicle of expression of Americans' attitudes, feelings, and emotions, and how these often relate to specific events and eras in the history of our nation.

Although the difference between the wording of the program theme and the wording of the educational objective is primarily one of perspective, the distinction is an important one. The wording of the educational objective puts the students and their learning at the center of the statement. It has more punch, in terms of using it in promotional copy or in discussing the program with school administrators, because it addresses the principal's concerns, in very specific terms, regarding what students will learn from seeing the program. The program theme serves as a tool to help determine what pieces, demonstrations, and activities should be included in the program and to determine a logical order for their presentation.

### The chicken or the egg?

It would be possible for an artist to develop from scratch, without any prior conceptions regarding what artistic content might be included, a program that would accomplish a given educational objective. This is often the best approach for artists developing a program that uses an art form as a medium for addressing a non-art educational theme. For example, a folk singer wishing to develop a program about substance abuse might first articulate the program theme—a program of songs, stories, and narrative designed to prevent drug abuse—and then begin the search for music, stories, facts, and figures to develop the theme. Most often though, artists go about it the other way around. Have an existing repertoire, they are looking for ways to put together a series of pieces or works in order to create a program. For example, in the program mentioned earlier featuring American folk music (a program my duo developed several years ago), we didn't come up with the educational objective first and then find the songs to match it. Rather, in analyzing our existing repertoire, we saw that there were many American folk songs and noticed that they expressed a wide variety of emotions. In addition, it occurred to us that many of the songs came out of specific historical contexts: the Civil War, the years of slavery, the Revolutionary War, the railroad building era, the Gold Rush, etc. It was only then that we had an idea of what students might learn from a program of American folk songs from our repertoire. We began to see that the program could be built around the various emotions expressed in the songs and the historical context that gave rise to those feelings. As we began assembling the songs, we realized there were some emotions and feelings, as well as some important historical eras, for which we had no songs. At this point, we switched approaches and began seeking program content that would address these specific theme areas. A tour through our song books and a few trips to the library provided the necessary material.

## A starting point

If, like most artists developing their first program, you do not have a preconceived idea your main program theme, get out some paper and, for each work or piece in your repertoire that has potential for inclusion in a performance for young people, write out answers to the following questions:

- who created the work, what country did they live in, and when was the work created?

- does the work exemplify, or highlight, the work of a particular person involved in the creation or presentation of the work (composer, choreographer, playwright, soloist, etc.)?

- does the work feature the use of a particular instrument, technique, backdrop, or piece of equipment?

- was there a significant historical context in which the work was created or first performed?

- does the work exemplify a particular style or genre within your art form?

- does the work illustrate in an obvious fashion one of the elements (examples: melody or rhythm in music, form or movement in dance, plot or action in theater) of your art form?

- is there a definite mood or feeling being expressed in the work or piece?

Depending on your discipline and repertoire, some of these questions will be more relevant than others. Likewise, there may be some additional aspects to be analyzed in each of the works or pieces.

After you have done this for each work in your repertoire, see if there are one or two of these questions for which there seems to be a wide range of answers from one piece to the next. For example, in looking through the answers to the question regarding the elements of your art form, you may discover that for each of the elements there are one or two pieces that exemplify the function of that particular element. If so, explaining the roles of the art form's elements represents a potential program theme. If you notice that these same works also represent several different styles or genres, illustrating how the use of these elements varies from one style to the next is a potential sub-theme.

Through the process of analyzing the pieces in your repertoire, you will discover possibilities for the development of one or more of the following themes:

● history of the art form

● styles and genres of the art form

● elements of the art form

● equipment, instruments, and tools required in the creation and presentation of works

● skills required to perform particular works

● roles played in the creation and presentation of works

● the expressive potential of the art form.

In the next several sections, we'll take a closer look at each of the above.

**Historical themes**

Art has always been influenced by the historical context from which it arises. Many works of art are commentaries, protests, or endorsements of events that took place in their creator's lifetime. Such works reflect the fact that they were written in times of war, defeat, victory, economic depression, political oppression, etc. Themes that make connections between artistic works and historical context offer considerable opportunity for making connections to classroom curriculum, particularly history. More on making these connections later.

**Themes of the art form's styles**

Program themes can serve to develop an understanding of an art form's various genres or styles. Pieces or works exemplifying the various genres within the art form comprise the artistic

23

content of the program while narratives, skits, and demonstrations help students understand what makes each style unique. This approach, by its very nature, leads to considerable contrast between the artistic selections—an important factor in holding students' attention. Often the pieces are put together in such a way that they also represent the art form's history and development, offering the possibility of further thematic development through the illustration of how new styles of the art form were influenced by previous styles.

## Themes of art form analysis

Breaking down an art form into its various elements is another popular program theme. In the discipline of music, for example, a program based on this theme would use performance pieces, activities, and narration to highlight the various elements of music: melody, harmony, rhythm, timbre. Likewise, theater artists would develop the elements of character, plot, action, and setting, while dance artists develop form, space, time, and movement. Because none of these elements occur in a vacuum within a work of art, isolating and providing an understanding of the function of each of the elements through the use of narration, skits, or demonstrations will provide a means by which students can begin watching or listening to performance pieces with a heightened awareness of how these elements work together.

## Themes of technology, hardware, and skills

Program themes or sub-themes can be based on the tools, instruments, and hardware used in the creation and presentation of an art form's works. For example: in music these would include the various instruments, the conductor's baton, the printed music and score; in theater, the backdrops, props, and lighting; in puppetry, the stage, the puppets, the strings and other controls. Presenting particular works that highlight specific technologies or hardware can demonstrate their role within the art form. In some cases, artists can demonstrate

24

how rudimentary tools, instruments, and hardware can be made by students at home or in class, allowing them to begin experimenting with the art form on their own.

Performers of circus arts and street arts presenting programs on juggling, unicycling, magic, and the like can also introduce students to the physical skills required in performing these acts: balance, eye-hand coordination, agility, etc. Students can gain insights into how they can begin developing these skills at home or in PE classes, empowering them to work toward what the artists have accomplished.

### Themes explaining creative roles

Programs can be designed to elucidate the roles played by people involved in the creation and presentation of an art form's works or pieces. With music, for example, the program might consist of a number of works, each providing a good example of the role of a particular creative person (composer, conductor, musician, etc.) while narratives, skits, and activities help students understand the playing out of each of the roles and their interrelated nature.

### Themes of the art form's expressive qualities

Programs can be developed that demonstrate an art form's potential for expression. Illustrating how the elements of the art form are manipulated in a particular work to express the feelings or moods is often a sub-theme of such programs. Another potential sub-theme is the illustration of the roles played by the creative people whose job is to accurately and effectively communicate the mood or feeling intended by the creator.

### All (or some) of the above

Working with a broader theme is often helpful for artists developing a program whose educational objective relates to the art form itself, especially when putting together a program for the first time. The broader the theme, the larger the pool of pieces or works to consider in selecting artistic content to develop that theme. Several of the previously discussed concepts can be incorporated into the theme. Such a theme might be stated as follows: an introduction to the history, composers, elements, instruments, expressive qualities, and presentation of classical music. A word of caution here: if the theme becomes too broad, the program will lack focus and clarity.

## Non-art themes

Art forms such as theater, vocal music, puppetry and storytelling, where the use of words is an integral part of the performance pieces, offer additional possibilities for program themes. Social themes such as abstaining from drug and alcohol use, environmental responsibility, non-violent problem solving, racial equality, and other issues may be addressed by using the art form as a medium for conveying the message. Such programs offer a bonus from a marketing perspective: principals will be exposing their students to an art form while at the same time reinforcing an important social message. Many schools have a topic-of-the-month program, addressing a number of these concepts over the course of a year. Principals often book programs that tie into the topic of the month.

The following themes are popular among administrators:

- drug-abuse prevention
- environmental responsibility
- self-esteem
- non-violent conflict resolution
- cultural diversity
- personal safety
- positive mental attitude
- personal responsibility & active citizenship.

In developing these types of programs, it is critical that you possess, or gain through research, expertise in the subject area at hand. This will help you find or create artistic material for the program. For example, a theater artist assembling or creating short, one-act works to develop a program on drug-abuse prevention will soon hit a dead end if she is under the impression that saying "No" to drugs is all there is to preventing drug abuse. On the other hand, many creative ideas for program content will be inspired by learning how issues such as self-esteem, quality of family life, peer pressure, and other social issues are related to drug abuse. Organizations such as the Center for Substance Abuse Prevention (see Appendix) can provide useful information at little or no cost. It is also a good idea to become knowledgeable on how existing in-school programs are presenting these issues to students in the grade levels for which you will be performing. This will prevent you from presenting conflicting perspectives that may raise objections from school counselors, parents, and teachers. In addition, this knowledge will give you the confidence to promote your program effectively, making connections between your message and their existing program. A consultation with a school counselor is a good place to begin in gaining this knowledge.

## Ethnic themes

Programs that expose students to various ethnic groups and their culture (Hispanic, African, Native American, and Asian themes are among the most popular) are often sought by principals. Multi-disciplined artists often include works from two or more art forms. For example, presenting the music and dance of an ethnic group, with instrument-making as a sub-theme, is a common theme. In many of these programs, backdrops and costuming create an authentic setting for the program. With these types of programs, the potential for making ties to grade-level curriculum is considerable.

## CREATING NON-PERFORMANCE CONTENT

Assuming that through analyzing your repertoire you have come up with a program theme and collection of works that will serve to develop that theme, it is now time to begin creating non-performance content (NPC) that will tie the works or pieces together. Simply performing the works and leaving it up to the kids to decipher what your program is all about will not suffice. NPC also serves as a means of engaging the audience by providing something specific to watch for or listen to in each piece. The following may be utilized as vehicles in conveying NPC to address program theme, illustrate concepts, or define terms:

- narration (speaking directly to the students)

- stage dialogue (conversation between members of an ensemble)

- audience dialogue (conversation between members of the ensemble and the audience)

- activities

- demonstrations

- skits

- stories.

In analyzing your repertoire, you discovered one or more common threads that linked together a number of pieces, leading to the emergence of a program theme and the determination of which pieces you would include in the presentation. Now, in moving on to the first step in the creation of NPC, your task is to explain, on paper, the connections between each of these pieces, the differences between each of the pieces, and how each piece relates to the theme. For example, let's say the theme of your program is the isolation of the various elements of music and the subsequent illumination of

28

the function of each of these elements. In the program, you will have one or two pieces that exemplify each of the primary elements of music (melody, harmony, rhythm, timbre). Begin the writing process by attempting to explain each of these elements of music in a way a nine-year-old would understand. What is melody? What would music be like without it? How does melody interact with the other elements of music? Having done this, write out an explanation of how the pieces you have chosen to demonstrate melody will do so. How will students be able to isolate the melody in the piece as it is played? By recognizing its melodic structure? By the instrument it is played on? Continue the writing process until the explanation of each element is smooth, concise, and represents something an elementary-school student would understand.

Through this process, you will end up with a series of narratives. Although you may ultimately use one or more of the other vehicles of NPC to convey the content of each of these narratives, creating concise narratives forces you to examine and articulate the following:

● how each piece in the proposed program specifically addresses some aspect of the program theme (This will help you determine if the piece truly belongs in the program and determine its logical place in the program order. Later, it will assist you in developing classroom preparation materials and creating a program description and outline for promotional purposes.)

● a definition of any special terms used in discussing the concept at hand.

### Translating narrative to other vehicles of NPC

Once you have created a narrative for each piece in your program, begin determining whether there are means other than the direct delivery of this narrative to convey the educational content of the narrative. Using a variety of vehicles to convey NPC makes the NPC segments more interesting and entertaining, and engages the audience. This, in turn, enhances student retention of the concepts addressed. The following is an example of how the information in the narrative dealing with the element of melody (discussed above) may be conveyed through the use of a combination of several other vehicles of NPC: A well known tune such as "Jingle Bells" is played with all the instruments playing in a monotone (a demonstration that serves to elucidate the concept of melody through its omission). Members of the ensemble begin discussing with one another why this piece just doesn't sound like "Jingle Bells." A member of the ensemble speculates that it is because the melody is missing. (The vehicle of stage dialogue has been introduced.) Another member of the ensemble indicates that she has no idea what *melody* means and asks students in the audience to raise their hands if they know what it means. (Audience dialogue has been incorporated.) As the students begin to formulate an explanation of the concept of melody, an ensemble member indicates that he thinks the ensemble could fully understand the concept of melody if the audience would first sing "Jingle Bells" using only one note, and then sing it again, using all the notes. (An activity involving the students has been implemented.) Now that the concept of melody has been dealt with in an entertaining way through this skit, a member of the ensemble plays the melody of the upcoming performance piece, explaining that this readily identifiable melody will occur throughout the performance, and asks the students to raise their hands every time it is repeated during the performance of the next piece. (A means of engaging the audience in actively listening to the piece has been introduced.)

While you may not want to present every thematic concept in this way, doing so occasionally will shake things up, avoiding predictability and the subsequent fragmentation of the audience's attention. Some artists may feel that involving themselves in such theatrics is above and beyond their talents, interests, and capabilities. For such artists, the above activity could be conducted in a more straightforward manner, excluding the pseudo-confusion among members of the ensemble over why the piece doesn't sound right.

## Using stories to convey NPC

The telling of stories to convey NPC is also very effective in engaging the audience. Stories work best when they are personalized. In the above-described program, the concept of tempo might be addressed in the following manner by a violinist relaying a story about the difficulty involved in playing passages at high speeds: Discussing how he has been working to get the piece "The Flight of the Bumble Bee" up to speed, the violinist explains how difficult it is to get the right hand synchronized with the left at such a fast tempo. Personalizing the story further, he brings out a metronome and indicates that it is a tool he uses in working on speed by starting at a slow tempo and gradually increasing the speed. Moving into demonstration, he sets the metronome to a relatively slow tempo and begins playing a passage. Afterwards, he moves the metronome setting up a bit and plays it again at a faster tempo. This cycle is repeated until he is playing at breakneck speed.

One of the programs my duo presents uses vocal music to develop a theme about taking care of the environment. As an explanation of the importance of the proper disposal of plastic bags and six-pack rings, my partner tells a story about how she was on a lake in a rowboat one day and came upon a duck who was flapping about in the water, unable to fly. As she rowed closer to it, she could see that one of its wings was ensnared in a plastic bag. Putting on gloves to avoid being bitten or pecked by the frantic bird, she was able to get the bag off the duck's wings, and it was able to fly away. She goes on to explain that while this story has a happy ending, many birds and animals die each year by getting caught in plastic litter. Every time she tells this story the room is completely quiet. Kids like the story so much that she is sometimes asked during Q&A at the end of the program to tell it again.

# Developing a Program

## Incorporating audience participation

*Plan segments of audience participation in advance—don't just decide that you have to have the audience participate and then pull something out of your hat. As you consider involving the audience in your program, first ask yourself how the activity will further your educational objective. Remember also, you don't have to troop large numbers of students up on the stage—just a couple will engage the entire audience.* - Nan Westervelt, Executive Director, Young Audiences of Rochester

So far, in developing a program, you have determined likely pieces to include, articulated a program theme, and created segments of NPC. Now it's time to think about audience participation. Perhaps you have already incorporated audience participation in skits, dialogues, activities, and other NPC segments. If not, you may want to take another look at these segments and see if there are ways of getting the audience involved.

There are two basic approaches to involving the audience: group participation and individual participation. In group participation, the entire audience participates from where they are seated. In individual participation, a single student (or a small group of students) is selected by the artist to come forward and participate with the artist or ensemble. There is considerable debate over which approach is better. Reviewing the panel containing quotes from interviews with principals (page 30), you will see that there are distinct pros and cons to each approach. Basically, it breaks down like this: group participation gives everyone in the audience an opportunity to participate, thus increasing retention of the material presented. On the other hand, because of the numbers involved, group participation can quickly become an audience-management problem for the artist. Individual participation greatly reduces the risk of losing control of the audience. On the down side, individual participation carries the risk of embarrassing the student, provides only a few students with an opportunity to participate, and presents the artist with the difficult task of

# Principals, on audience participation

*There is more risk involved when students are called forward. If it's done gratuitously, those kids can be put on the spot in a negative way. If your presentation allows, I think it's good to get the whole group involved—let everybody have a chance to participate in some way.* - Cory Crawford, Fruitland ES, Puyallup WA

*I think it's easier to manage participation when a small group of kids is brought forward rather than the whole group participating. The question with whole-group participation is whether or not you can get them refocused. I've had a couple of disasters where once the presenters got the kids energized they couldn't de-energize them. It's one of the most common audience-control errors I see. Have a strategy to get them grounded again—a cue or signal worked out in advance—because it will affect the rest of the performance if you can't get them refocused.* - Tim O'Brien, Issaquah Valley ES, Issaquah WA

*Audience participation that involves singling out students tends to get everyone silly and giddy. One or two students get to participate but the others don't. It's more educational, and the students will retain a lot more of what is being taught, when they are all participating. Individual participation is also a risk because the performers usually have no idea which kids to pick. We, as teachers, are all thinking, "Oh no! Who are they going to pick? They just can't pick Charlie—it'll bomb if they pick Charlie." Choosing teachers to come forward also provides a lot of fear and stress: they don't like being called up front and used as clowns.* - Brian Fox, Karshner ES, Puyallup WA

*Little kids love to see their teachers and/or principal be involved in a show. But a word of forewarning: prior to the assembly, make sure that is all up front. I had a group in here once that kind of picked on the teachers, and they really resented it. I haven't had them back.* - Jim Eisenhardt, Yelm Prairie ES, Yelm WA

*I think you are always at risk when you get the audience involved. It's just like when you try to do something crazy in the classroom: you're at risk of taking them to the edge and not being able to get them back. I like to see performers take the risk, but it can make or break the program.* - Venita Ellick, Gordon ES, Kingston WA

33

selecting students who are capable of doing what they will be asked to do.

Both approaches have a time and place. Assuming that you are skilled at managing the audience, use individual participation when the very nature of the activity precludes the possibility of group participation, such as having a student play an instrument with the ensemble, act out a simple role, participate in a way that requires significant physical movement, or assist in a demonstration. In activities where it is practical for the entire audience to participate, don't limit the participation activity to one or two students; use group participation.

When considering individual participation, make sure the rest of the audience will learn something while observing the volunteer participant. Having a student come up on stage and play a simple instrument with the ensemble while the other kids simply watch is not a valid participation activity. However, if the concept at hand is the technique of improvisation, and the participation activity is designed to show how anyone's improvisation, by its very nature, is not right or wrong, and the the selected student will demonstrate this by improvising on the instrument (illustrating how whatever they play goes along quite nicely with what the rest of the band is doing), then the audience will learn something about improvisation as they watch.

In planning a group participation activity, create and memorize a script providing very specific instructions for the audience; this is no time to wing it. You must let the audience know in advance what you want them to do and how you want them to do it. If the activity is physical, remind them of the importance of staying within their own space. Remind them that there are hundreds of people in the room and to think about personal responsibility and safety. Remind them that there should be no talking, only listening and participation.

Follow up a participation activity with something that will refocus the audience quickly—an up-tempo song to which everybody claps their hands; a flashy, visual piece; the introduction of a new, fascinating character or puppet. It's best if the following segment is something that will not be seriously impeded by a little commotion as the participating students return to their seats or the audience in general gets itself settled back in and returns to a spectator mode, both mentally and physically. Don't plan to deliver a long narrative or begin a dialogue at this point. You want to avoid standing at the microphone for five minutes, asking the audience to quiet down; it makes both you and the audience look bad.

You can place participation activities almost anywhere in the program order except the very beginning; the kids will need a few minutes to get to know you and become comfortable with you.

You will find specific examples of audience participation activities in Part Two in the program descriptions and observation reports.

### Involving the teachers in participation

Before we leave the subject of participation, a word about involving teachers in participation activities. Teachers do not appreciate being used as laughingstocks. It seems ridiculous to state something so seemingly obvious, but I have seen artists on several occasions use teachers to entertain the kids in a less-than-respectful way. For example, I was recently involved in the following incident while observing a program: The leader of the ensemble indicates that she wants all staff members to come forward. Not knowing what to expect (remember to always demonstrate the activity first before bringing participants up), the teachers are reluctant, but gradually begin trudging up to the front of the room. Pointing me out and addressing me through the microphone—she is assuming that I am a teacher—she beckons me to come up as well. Not wanting to make a scene by indicating that I am just a visitor, I go. (Never put anyone in the audience on the spot in such a manner. For all she knew, I was handicapped or had a bladder control problem. How would I have felt blurting this out?) She tells the kids that the teachers are going to look funny, but not to laugh until the end, at which time everyone will laugh at them together. Getting us into a line, she demonstrates, one at a time, several different steps or movements to a line dance. Finally she has us put it all together, doing the dance to the ensemble's accompaniment. Several of the steps require us to move our bodies in ways that make us feel foolish. At the end of the dance, the leader says, "Let's give the teachers a hand. It's not easy to come up here and make a fool out of yourself." (Never portray participating with the ensemble as something foolish, embarrassing, or humiliating. Make it seem like an honor. Validate the participants efforts afterwards.)

If you are planning to involve teachers in participation, make it voluntary: don't pressure them or simply point them out and ask them to come forward. Make sure that the activity in which you are going to involve them does not deprive them of their dignity. Don't use them as the butt of a lame attempt to add humor to the show.

## Half-time

There is some debate among artists over whether or not there ought to be a break midway through the program. Some argue that a break presents the artist with the difficult task of refocusing the audience's attention when it comes time for the show to resume, disrupts the continuity of the show, and is not really necessary as far as the kids are concerned. I disagree. In our programs there is always a break about two-thirds of the way through the show for the following reasons: One, it gives the teachers an opportunity to move students who are having a difficult time focusing on the show to a location where they will be less distracting to you and the rest of the audience; two, I have repeatedly overheard kids express appreciation for the fact that they were granted an opportunity to get off the hard floor for a couple of moments; and three, I have received nothing but positive feedback from administrators regarding the inclusion of the break. Conversely, I often hear negative comments about artists who expect first-graders to sit on the hard floor for 45 minutes without a break. Potential audience-management difficulties can be avoided by providing clear instructions before you have the students stand up, prearranging a sign or signal indicating when it's time to sit down again, and by following the break with an engaging performance or NPC activity that will not be hampered by a little noise from the audience as they get reseated. For example, when announcing the break, I say:

I know that many of you have been sitting on the hard floor for more than half an hour and that can get pretty uncomfortable [remember, many of the kids will be seated on the floor for ten minutes or more before your show begins, and usually these are the youngest since the little ones sit up front and must come in first], so here's what we're going to do: In just a moment, not quite yet though, I'm going to give you a chance to stand up and stretch your legs. But before we do that, I'm going to ask you to use only very gentle voices while you're up so that you can still hear [always give a reason for a request such as this], and as soon as you hear Cindy and me begin singing the next song—a song that you are going to recognize—we would like you to sit back down as quickly and quietly as possible and begin singing with us. [A signal other than hollering "Sit down!" has been prearranged.] And when you sit back down, we'd like you to make sure you're sitting flat on your bottoms [yes, this word is OK, we've never gotten so much as a snicker] so it will be easier for those behind you to see well. So please remember those things. I'm sure you'll have no problem because you have already shown that you are a great audience, very good at following instructions. [I take the opportunity here to praise them for their accomplishments thus far and show expectation that they will continue to succeed.] So if you'd like to, go ahead and stand up for a moment and stretch your legs.

The song we go into at the end of the break is always one the audience knows and loves. By the end of the first few bars, ninety-five percent of the students are back down and singing. Between the end of the refrain and the upcoming verse (as we continue to play the guitars, covering up the seam here), I praise them for doing a great job and indicate that I am going to wait just a moment for students who are still getting settled to bring their attention up front. This brings the stragglers into line, and then we go on with the song. I know from the instances where the show started late and we decided to eliminate the break to save time that the students' ability to remain focused through the end of the program is greatly reduced without the break.

Instead of a designated break, it is possible for the objective of the break to be accomplished through an NPC activity that gets the kids off the floor. However, there is no opportunity here for teachers to deal with kids who may be out in the middle of the room distracting other students with less-than-desirable behavior. Teachers, afraid of creating an even bigger distraction, are often reluctant to walk out in the middle of the room and address such situations while your show is going on. Furthermore, if you are on tour performing four or five shows a day, *you* need the break. A chance to get a quick drink of water, communicate something to your partner, tune that damned B-string, or move your hands and body from a cramped position can make all the difference in coaxing from your inner reserves the energy necessary to make it through the rest of the tour.

## DETERMINING THE PROGRAM ORDER

A most challenging task in developing a program is deciding on the most logical progression of the components of the program. The following are some considerations:

- developing the educational objective so that one concept builds upon another

38

- pacing the program so the heavier material is at the beginning of the program and the lighter material toward the end

- strategically placing the occurrences of activities, demonstrations, skits, audience participation, and other non-performance content

- making smooth transitions from one program component to the next

- arranging for contrast between the works or pieces

- alternating which member of the ensemble is featured in the work or conducts the NPC related to the work (Such alternating will help maintain the audience's interest and—in cases where the performances are physically demanding—help regulate energy expenditure.)

- allowing for the addressing of technical needs such as costume changes, set changes, instrument retuning, equipment adjustments, etc.

- identifying both a strong beginning and ending piece.

The list of considerations will, of course, vary with each art form, artist, and repertoire. Finding an order that is perfect in every way is impossible. Often, when you change the order to address one area of consideration, the change completely destroys the sequencing of the others. There will be instances where you will have no choice but to compromise the sequencing of one area of consideration in order to optimize another.

**Using 3x5 index cards**

Figure 3-1 illustrates how you can indicate on a 3x5 index card all the pertinent considerations for a proposed piece or work. The card in the illustration is based on cards used to determine the order for the program of American folk songs discussed earlier in this chapter. Having a card for each work—with the same indications in the same area of each card—will allow you to quickly lay out many different orders

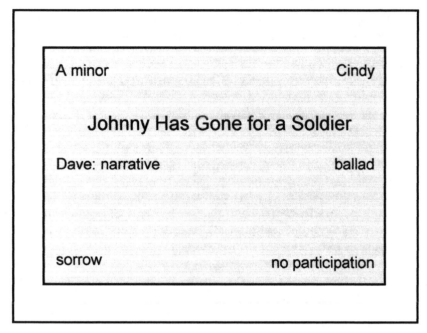

**Figure 3-1:** Example of a song card used in determining program order. Moving clockwise, the upper left-hand corner indicates the key, upper right-hand corner indicates the featured singer, mid-height on right-hand side indicates the tempo of the song, lower right-hand corner is for notes on audience participation, lower left-hand corner indicates the feeling communicated in the song, mid-height on left-hand side indicates the nature of any non-performance content related to the song.

Making one of these cards (3x5 index cards work well) for each proposed piece or work, with the indications in the same area of each card, will make it easier to check the sequencing of various aspects of the pieces as you rearrange the order over and over, attempting to come up with the best possible program set.

and see at a glance how the new order affects the sequencing of each of the considerations. If you're lucky, you'll find an order that allows for a good sequencing of all the areas of consideration. More likely though, you'll discover that there seems to be no particular order that meets the needs of all the areas of consideration. You may find that when you come up with an order that allows for good contrast between the pieces, there are three numbers in the very beginning containing audience participation, while there is no participation for the rest of the program. The list of potential problems is endless. To solve the problems, you may have to make some fundamental changes regarding repertoire and NPC. You may have to forget about the participation you had planned on certain numbers and work some participation into pieces where you were not planning to involve the audience. You may have to drop one of the works or pieces and find a new one that fits the specific requirements of the slot left open by its removal. You just have to keep tinkering with it until you've got it. It can take days—even more if you have to find new pieces, create new segments of NPC, or make other significant changes. And if that's not intimidating enough, remember that after you actually perform the set for the first time, you'll likely be spending some time with the cards once again. On the bright side, once you've got it, you'll be performing the set over and over, polishing and perfecting it until it is truly a work of art.

## Openers and closers

*Start with something that is appealing to all the senses and gets the kids' attention right away, rather than talking for several minutes and having everyone waiting for an actual performance. Afterwards, you can address audience expectations and other things necessary for the material being presented.* -Brian Fox, Principal, Karshner ES, Puyallup WA

There is a general feeling among administrators and artists alike that the opener should be something flashy and attention getting. However, some artists and their programs may not, by their very nature, be flashy. Being such an artist myself, I know the fallacy of trying to be flashy when you're just not flashy.

41

Also, in my programs, I present myself more as an educator using music as a medium for education than an entertainer, and educators are not under such pressure to be flashy. So if being flashy is not for you, don't despair. It is possible to be immediately engaging, for example, simply by being genuinely warm and personable (consider the popular TV personality, Mr. Rogers). You can also begin with an entertaining story about something that happened on the way to the school or an enthusiastic introduction of what your program is all about.

There is less consensus between artists and administrators over closers. Artists tend to think the closer should be a real show-stopper, while many administrators feel this kind of closing creates a student management problem for both themselves and the teachers: the kids can get so jacked up that it's hard to get them organized for the return trip to their classrooms. Remember, at the end of the show you will be handing the kids over—in whatever state you left them—to the principal. She must now get their attention and give instructions for dismissal. Even though it's going to run against your grain as a performer, consider doing something more subdued for a closer. In one of my duo's programs, we lead the kids in a fade-out on the final refrain of the last song. Just before the last time through, when we do it at a whisper, we thank them (in a very soft voice, keeping with the fade-out theme) for being a great audience, tell them to remain seated after the program is over, and ask them to give their full attention to the principal as she gives them instructions for dismissal. By doing this, we have made the principal's job immensely easier.

## Pacing

*Especially with younger kids, you've got to keep it moving because their attention span is so short...We're competing with "Sesame Street"—think about how quickly the show moves from one type of thing to the next. It's more than just varying the performance numbers: move from talking to music to participation to demonstrations.* - Venita Ellick, Principal, Gordon ES, Kingston WA

The sequencing and placement of performance pieces and segments of NPC will affect both audience focus and student retention of the educational content of the program. Strive for both variety and logical progression. Variety will keep the audience focused, and logical progression will serve the educational objective.

Place the bulk of the educational content between the first five minutes and the last ten minutes of the program. In the first five minutes of the program, the student's attention will be focused on who you are, what you look like, what you sound like, and spirit and flavor of the program. After thirty minutes, the outer limits of students' attention span will be rapidly approaching. Beyond this point, quicken the pace, keeping performance numbers and segments of NPC short, fun, and entertaining.

**Covering seams**

To keep the audience focused, plan for smooth transitions from one work or piece (and its related NPC) to the next. For example, if a violinist needs to switch to a viola for the next number, have other members of the ensemble conducting an activity, demonstration, or other NPC at that time. Don't think for a minute that she can put away the violin, go get the viola, open the case, take out the new instrument, tighten and rosin the bow, check the intonation, and return to her seat—all this in full view of the audience—and have anyone in the audience pay a bit of attention to a narrative or dialogue. The only thing the students will have learned during those few moments is how one puts away a violin and takes out a viola. Follow these guidelines as much as possible in covering seams:

- minimize the movements and time involved in the distracting activity as much as possible by advance planning

- whenever possible, go behind a curtain or screen as soon as the previous piece ends, conduct the activity out of sight of the students, and don't return until the activities being conducted by the rest of the ensemble are finished and it is time to begin the next piece

- whenever the performance of a piece or the conducting of an NPC activity must compete with a distracting activity conducted by another member of the ensemble, upstage the distracting activity by making the performance or NPC something as engaging and attention getting as possible.

Never let a situation occur where the entire ensemble goes about rearranging sets, adjusting equipment, changing costumes, etc., while the kids are left waiting for the show to resume. A few moments of such *dead airspace* can put the audience into a state from which it will take several minutes to coax them back.

## Making connections to grade-level curriculum

Once you have decided on a program order, you can begin thinking about making connections between the educational content of your program and the students' classroom curriculum. While this step is optional, such connections will enhance the educational value of your program and, when stated in your promotional materials, help convince school administrators of the educational merit of your program.

Call your state's Department of Education and ask how you may obtain information outlining the requirements for each grade level. Some states are *local control* states, meaning that while there are general state guidelines for curriculum, it is left up to the local districts to determine the specific areas of study for each grade level. If your state is in this category, contact one of the larger school districts in the state and ask them for their curriculum guidelines. Most districts within the state will adhere to roughly the same agenda. Looking through these publications, you may discover academic requirements to which your program is relevant. For example, an artist doing a program on American folk music may see that fourth-grade students are required to study U.S. History; an artist doing a program on Native American culture may find fifth-graders are currently touching on this in State History; an artist doing a program on the elements of music may find that students in the sixth grade are dealing with that same topic in Music.

The following are specific learning requirements excerpted from the guidelines of a major school district in Washington state. Each of them is an example of a classroom curriculum requirement to which the content of assembly programs might be connected:

● Third-grade PE: students will develop an ability to perform movements to music.

● Fourth-grade Music: students will understand the nature of the percussion family's voicings.

● Fifth-grade Science: Students will develop an understanding of the earth, weather, and how people affect the environment and space beyond the solar system.

● Sixth-grade Social Studies: Students will develop an understanding of the culture, art, and history of Africa.

Usually curriculum connections will be addressed by classroom teachers—with the help of the study guides you will provide for them—in the classroom before or after the show. Trying to make connections during the show (except in a very general way) can have you going too many directions at once in the forty-minute course of your program.

### Creating classroom-preparation materials

*Some of the teachers won't use classroom-preparation material at all. There's so much on the teacher's plate already...I can recall, when I was in the classroom, if the material represented a lot of information and took too much time to read through, I wouldn't get to it. If it was a one-sheet, here-are-three-things-you-can-discuss-with-your-kids-before-going-to-the-assembly kind of thing or a simple activity, then I would use it...If it's going to be an activity, make it involve materials that are available in the classroom already, not*

Study Guide for the assembly program,
**The Elements of Music**

**Program Description**: The Nelson String Quartet will present a program of classical works that will help students understand the function of the four basic elements of music: melody, rhythm, timbre, and harmony. These elements may be described as follows:

Melody: The aspect of music to which you can whistle or hum.

Rhythm: The aspect of music to which you can clap your hands or tap your feet.

Timbre: The aspect of music that makes one instrument sound different from another. For example, you can tell the difference between a flute and a trumpet because of the difference in their timbres.

Harmony: Harmony exists when two or more instruments are playing notes at the same time.

**NOTE:** Sixth-grade students are currently studying the elements of music in music classes.

Other terms that will be used in the program include the following:

Solo: When an instrument is featured by itself in the playing of a passage.

Duet: When two instruments are featured together in the playing of a passage.

**Audience Expectations:**

1. Students should not talk at any time during the program unless called upon by one of the performers.

2. Students should sit on the floor with their legs crossed and their hands in their own personal space.

Figure 3-2: A simple study guide for a music presentation with a theme that addresses the four elements of music.

*something that you have to go out and hunt down.* - Brian Fox, Principal, Karshner ES, Puyallup WA

The key to developing preparation materials that will actually be used is making them brief, organized, and simple. Include the following information:

- the overall theme of your program

- three or four basic concepts you will be addressing in the development of that theme

- connections to classroom curriculum

- definitions of any special terms you will be using in the presentation

- a concise description of the show (Let the students know whether they can expect a puppet show or rock concert.)

- guidelines for appropriate audience behavior for your program.

If you wish to include detailed instructions regarding discussions, activities, and exercises in your preparation materials and do not have classroom experience or training, work with an educator in developing those materials. Several versions of such detailed materials will have to be prepared in order for them to be appropriate for each grade level.

Figure 3-2 provides an example of a simple study guide.

**Testing your program**

After you have developed a program and prepared some simple study guides, arrange for some trial performances. If you live near a large school district, make contact with the district-level coordinator for music curriculum and see if you can make arrangements for a series of performances within the district. If there is no music coordinator, talk with the superintendent. Offer to trade free performances for evaluation from staff. Arrange visits to classrooms after the shows and get some direct feedback from the students. Discuss your study guides with teachers. This will give you an opportunity to work the bugs out of the show, improve the study guides, and get comfortable with presenting in the school environment.

## Some advice on advice

One of the most difficult aspects of reviewing evaluations and suggestions is separating the chaff from the grain. The designing of a program is a very intricate process. Many of the imperfections in a program exist not because their existence escaped the artist, but because it is sometimes necessary to allow an imperfection in one area in order to solve a larger problem somewhere else. Sometimes you'll be advised to do something that, as far as you're concerned, seems totally out of the question. When this happens, strive for the courage and honesty to determine whether the suggestion represents something incompatible with your personality or your identity as an artist, or something you are simply afraid to try.

## Summary

The steps in developing an assembly program are as follows:

1. Analysis of your repertoire and the subsequent discovery of a program theme (In some situations the theme is articulated first, followed by a search for supporting repertoire.)

2. Preliminary selection of the works or pieces that best address the program theme

3. Creation of NPC, beginning with the writing of narratives, to tie the works together

4. Translating the narratives to other vehicles of NPC

5. Incorporation of audience participation

6. Determination of the program order

7. The search for curriculum connections

8. Preparation of classroom study guides

9. Testing the program.

The sequence of the above steps is not always rigidly adhered to. In many instances you'll find yourself jumping from one step to another as new ideas occur to you. The process is often more circular than linear.

See Chapter 11, an interview with the Director of Program Development for National Young Audiences, for additional information on program design.

# CHAPTER 4
# Marketing & Promotion

This chapter is designed to provide assistance in tailoring the basic concepts of promotion to the school market. It is assumed that the reader has experience in creating and utilizing promotional materials. The provision of detailed information on the science of marketing, writing effective promotional copy, or the creation of specific promotional pieces is beyond the scope of this book. If you need assistance in these areas, supplemental publications are available from the publisher. See the order form at the back of the book for more information.

There are several means of acquiring bookings for school performances, including the following:

● working with booking agencies

● working with private organizations such as *Young Audiences*

● working with arts commissions

● independently promoting your program.

In the first sections of this chapter, we'll take a look at each of these options.

## Booking agencies

Private booking agencies sometimes book their artists in schools. However, since an agent's primary motive is to make money through commissions, they generally work only with large, well-established ensembles capable of commanding a large fee. For most artists on their rosters, performing in schools is a sideline activity serving as a means of supplementing income from concerts and other performances.

For contact information on agencies in your area, look in the phone book under *agencies* or *entertainment*.

## Young Audiences, Inc.

Young Audiences is a national organization specializing in bringing performing artists to schools. While they are a non-profit organization, they do take a percentage of the artists' fees in order to cover their overhead. YA offers real opportunity for artists interested in specializing in school performances. Local chapters send out rosters to area schools and work one-on-one with principals and other contact persons, actively booking their artists for residencies, workshops, and assembly programs. While some YA artists send out supplemental promotion, many rely solely on YA personnel to handle the booking processes. YA operates chapters in all areas of the country. See the Appendix for contact information.

## Arts commissions

Many arts commissions have programs that sponsor performances in schools. Though some commissions will actually book tours for participating artists, in most programs, once accepted, artists will simply be included in a roster sent to the schools at the commission's expense. Interested schools will then review the roster, select artists they wish to book, and contact those artists independently to complete the booking. Once the artist and the school have worked out the details, the school must then apply to the commission for financial assistance in paying the artist's fee. Most arts commissions operate on a *subsidized fee* basis, paying a portion (usually 50%) of the fee, while the school pays the balance.

Typically, the number of bookings generated through the commission's roster alone is not great. Much better results are obtained when artists follow the commission's roster with their own promo, making reference to the fact that they have been accepted by the commission and explaining that their program is therefore eligible for funding support.

There are arts commissions operating on several levels. Each state has its own arts commission, which is usually located in the state capitol. You can obtain a nation-wide directory of state arts commissions through the National Assembly of State Arts Commissions (see Appendix). Larger counties and cities often have a commission as well. Many state commissions publish a directory of local county and city commissions operating within the state.

After obtaining contact information for the commissions in your area, inquire as to whether they have a program sponsoring performances in schools, a touring program, or an arts-in-education program. These are usually separate programs; request an application form for each. Most commissions are very strict about application deadlines. Have applications completed and in the mail well in advance of the deadline given in the instructions.

If you are accepted into a program, determine whether the commission handles the booking process or if they direct interested schools to contact the artists individually. If the commission does not handle the booking process and you wish to supplement the roster with your own promotion, obtain answers to the following questions:

- when do they send out their roster?

- do schools contract with the commission or with the artists?

- what percentage of your fee does the commission pay?

- what is the current funding period for the fee-subsidy program?

- what procedure and time frame must the schools adhere to in applying for commission funding support?

- will you receive a check from the school for the whole fee, a check from the commission for the whole fee, or two checks—one from the school and one from the commission?

- how many days after the performance can you expect to get paid?

With answers to these questions, you will be able to more effectively design your promotion and follow-up materials.

If you do not get accepted into any of the programs you apply for, do not be discouraged, especially if you are just getting started in the field. Competition is pretty fierce. You can still design and implement your own promotion plan and book yourself independently.

## Self-promotion

For artists interested in making serious income through performing in schools, self-promotion is an absolute necessity. Even if you're working with arts commissions and other presenting organizations, you'll find it necessary to supplement their promotional activities in order to maximize the number of bookings attained. My duo—even when on the rosters of four separate arts-commission programs at the same time—never received more than 30 percent of our bookings through commissions: we still obtained most of our work through independent promotion.

The steps taken in the process of self-promotion are as follows:

1. Obtaining mail lists for the areas in which you wish to promote your program

2. Creating the promotional package

3. Qualifying prospects by phone before sending a promotional package (optional)

4. Delivering or mailing the promotional packages

5. Making follow-up phone calls (optional)

6. Scheduling and confirming bookings.

The next sections will examine each of these steps.

## Obtaining mail lists

All states publish a directory of public schools. These directories can usually be obtained for ten or fifteen dollars from the state's Department of Education. Call the Department of Education (almost always located in the state capitol) to order a directory. Some states also have available mail lists printed on label format; these are usually considerably more expensive than the directory, but save you the time required to type the mail list. Usually lists purchased in label format can be selectively built (drawing from the commission's computer database), based on such factors as grade level, number of students, geographical location, etc. If you are planning to send your promotion via bulk mail, have the list sorted by zip code.

Mail lists in label format are also available from commercial list brokers. When ordering the list, you must decide who you want to direct the promotion to—the principal, the PTA, the assembly coordinator, the music teacher, etc.—in order to determine the top line of the labels. If you decide to direct your promotion to the principal, the broker should be able to include the principal's name as the top line of the label. However, if you choose one of the other options, the top line will contain only the job title. See the Appendix for a list of brokers who handle school mail lists.

If you are planning to prequalify prospects through telephone calls, you'll still need a copy of the Department of Education's directory—in addition to any preprinted lists you purchase—for the phone numbers.

## CREATING THE PROMOTIONAL PACKAGE

### Promotion formats

A brochure accompanied by a cover letter is probably the most common format for marketing to schools. This combination has the advantages of low printing costs and low mailing costs. Its primary disadvantage is that every time you need to make a simple change in the copy, the change must be made on the original master by the designer or typesetter (unless you're proficient with desktop publishing programs), and new copies must be run off and folded. This makes changes in copy more difficult and time consuming. Also, because this format is so common, your brochure will not stand out from the hundreds of other brochures schools receive annually.

A folder format, where an outer jacket resembling a *Pee-Chee* is used to contain several inner sheets, is another option. Advantages here are a bigger initial impact and the ability to make changes to the inner pages quickly, since they are often created on a personal typewriter or word-processing program. Printing the new copies is also relatively inexpensive, since they are usually printed in a single color on one side of an 8½ x 11 sheet of paper. Disadvantages include a high initial production cost, the considerable time required to assemble the folders, and a high mailing cost when shipping first class. You can reduce the cost for the jackets by running large quantities since they contain no copy requiring frequent changes—usually a photograph on the front and return address on the back.

### Information to include in promotional pieces

Promotional pieces sent to schools should include the following information:

- biographical information
- a photograph of the artist(s)
- descriptions of the programs you're offering
- staging or equipment requirements
- program fee
- recommendations
- a list of schools where you have performed
- schedule and booking information.

School administrators are very busy people. Spend some time editing and re-editing your work. Try to get each point across in the fewest possible words. Set the piece up in such a way that prospects immediately get an idea of what you are offering. Have information categorized in such a way that it is readily indexed by the reader: make it easy to skip some sections and concentrate on others.

## Biographical information

You'll remember from Chapter 1 that a principal has two primary concerns—the educational merit of your program and your ability to effectively present the program to elementary students. Begin addressing these concerns in your biographical information. Include any and all experience you have performing for children, and probably more importantly, any classroom or teaching experience you may have. If you've been accepted into art-in-education programs, mention these as well; participation in such programs represents an endorsement of your ability to educate as well as perform.

## The photograph

*If there is a "negative" in the picture it will draw my attention right away—anything suggestive, extreme, flamboyant, or offensive to any of our community members, particularly in an ethnic way. Most principals tend to be conservative, and they take a very conservative position when they bring outside programs into their schools, because many of us have very conservative communities.* - Newt Adams, Principal, Clarkmoor ES, Tacoma WA

Enough said.

## Program descriptions

Program descriptions may be written either in paragraph form, outline form, or both. In the former, the program is described in a short paragraph, providing the reader with a general idea of the content. Include the educational objective of the program and describe how the works and NPC accomplish the objective. Incorporate phrases that let the reader know you are in touch with the need to keep the kids engaged, participating, and focused.

A description written in outline format provides a chronological account of the development of the program theme, often supplying specific names of works included in the program and describing key segments of NPC. Figure 4-1 provides an example of combining description and outline formats.

### Staging and equipment requirements

Include any special needs you have regarding stages, dressing rooms, lighting or sound equipment. Be specific about these needs, but try to show flexibility at the same time; you don't want to come across as demanding and temperamental. Because many schools have poor performing facilities and equipment and are unable to meet all but the most basic of needs, having stringent equipment requirements seriously limits the number of schools that can book your program.

### Your fee

Program fees vary widely. There are single artists who charge as little as $75 and others who charge almost $1000. Duos range from $150 to over $1000. Ironically, artists whose

*Folk Music in America* is a fun, fast paced program. In this overview of American folk music, students will learn that American folk music is a vehicle of expression for a broad range of feelings and emotions, often stemming from specific events and eras in the history of our nation. Students participate throughout the program by singing, clapping and signing American Sign Language. Humorous skits develop concepts in a fun and entertaining way. Study guides and refrains to key songs are sent to the school several weeks in advance to enhance student participation during the program. The section-by-section outline below includes key songs and program content.

I.  **Patriotic songs** expressing Americans' love for their country, including *My Country 'tis of Thee* and *America the Beautiful.* Narrative and dialogue discuss the historical background of these beloved songs.

II. **Songs of war and peace,** including *When Johnny Comes Marching Home Again* and *Down by the Riverside.*

III. **Work songs,** including *Drill ye Terriers, Drill.* A humorous skit takes a look at the origin and meaning of the term *terrier* as it applies to railroad workers. A short story provides a historical context for the song.

IV. **Songs of play and fantasy,** including *Puff the Magic Dragon* and *I Don't Want to Play in Your Yard.* A skit helps students understand the terms *solo* and *duet.*

V.  **Songs about animals,** including *The Sow Got the Measles* and *A Place in the Choir.* Just for fun!

Figure 4-1: A program description utilizing both paragraph and outline formats.

income is derived solely from performing in schools generally charge less than those who present such performances in addition to working a conventional job. This makes sense when you think about it. Artists relying on school performances to make a living have to perform a hundred or more shows every year. They must adopt the *Wal-Mart* approach—low price, high volume—to get enough work to fill the calendar. Those who work conventional jobs are less concerned about losing a booking because their fee is too high; they have other income to rely on.

If you're just entering the school market, charge a fee at the lower end of the spectrum; you'll be competing with established acts. You can always raise your fee later as you build your reputation and increase the demand for your program.

In your promotional package, state your fee clearly. Studies show that when products or services are advertised without an indication of cost, response is diminished. Do not state that your fee is *negotiable*. Avoid attaching variables such as travel and lodging charges. If you are offering several services or combinations of services, design a fee schedule listing the fees individually. Prospects want to know, before they call, what the service is going to cost.

Most schools expect a substantially reduced fee (half price or less) for a second show. The rationale is that, although you'll be performing twice, you'll only have to set up and tear down once. In reality, this is true only if both shows are in the morning or if both shows are in the afternoon. If one show is in the morning and the other in the afternoon, you'll likely end up setting up and tearing down twice because the lunchroom and the auditorium are one and the same, and your equipment will be at considerable risk if left up during lunch time. If you decide to offer a discount for a second show—most artists do—specify that both shows must be scheduled in the morning or both in the afternoon.

If the schools are within the jurisdiction of an arts commission

# Principal Insights on Promotion

*I put a big emphasis on letters of recommendation from principals, especially if they are from someone I know...I am very influenced by recommendations I hear at a principals meeting or some similar forum.*

*I tend, as much as I can, to set up the assembly schedule by late summer because many of the assemblies are funded by the PTA, and I need to get the budget set for the year. I will leave a little room so that if later I find something that I really want to bring in, I can...Try to avoid sending promo when schools are closed for holidays because, when I come back, I have got just a mound of mail, and I tend not to look at it as carefully as when I have a smaller stack to go through.* - Newt Adams, Clarkmoor ES, Tacoma WA

*One of the driving forces leading up to the booking of an assembly is the PTA. Principals don't have time to be the sole coordinators for those types of things. In the springtime, the PTA is beginning to make decisions on next year's programs...things then get fully nailed down in August. Throughout the year I'll get many more promotions; I take those things as they come and often merge some of them into the existing schedule.* - Cory Crawford, Fruitland ES, Puyallup WA

*I don't know that I'm particularly swayed by the fact that an artist is sponsored by some presenting organization, but if an artist has several presenting organizations behind them, then that says to me that they are well thought of.* - Venita Ellick, Gordon ES, Kingston WA

*I am very unlikely to bring in a group if I have not seen them or if there is no one I can call to get an opinion. One of the first things I do is scan the material to see if there is a school in our district or county where they have been.* - Brian Fox, Karshner ES, Puyallup WA

*We put the most weight on letters of recommendation from other principals and a list of schools the artists have worked in. We're mostly looking to see if they know how to do a program in schools...I'm reluctant if there is no information on what they've done before in schools.* - Tim O'Brien, Issaquah Valley ES, Issaquah WA

you are working with, let the prospect know what percentage of your fee the commission will cover and the procedure they must follow in applying for the subsidy. Be prepared to offer assistance in obtaining and filling out the necessary application forms. Be absolutely certain of the accuracy of any statements you make regarding the commission's eligibility requirements, fee subsidy, or application procedures.

## Recommendations

Looking at the panel of excerpts from interviews (page 58), you can see that recommendations from principals are the most influential component of the promotional package. You can pull key lines from several letters and create a collage of quotes, saving space and sparing the reader from wading through extraneous verbiage to get to the punch lines. If you acquire a real gem of a letter, lauding your talents in several specific areas, presenting the letter in its entirety can be very effective. Whenever possible, quote principals from the same districts or areas in which you are promoting; this will give the recommendations more credibility and persuasiveness.

Letters that are specific in their praise of your ability to keep the audience engaged, educate as you entertain, and manage a large group of children are far more effective than letters of a more general nature stating that your program is "good" or "worthwhile." When asking for a letter of recommendation, you will be much more likely to acquire an effective one if you indicate specific areas you would like addressed. For example, if you need a letter attesting to your ability to manage a student audience, you might say in your request: "I am currently planning a tour of California. I know the principals in these schools, not being familiar with me or my program, will be concerned about my ability to educate and manage a large group of students. If there is anything you can say in this regard, I'm sure it will be very helpful in convincing them of the value of my program."

## A list of schools

After you have performed in a number of schools, begin including a section in your promotion listing the names of these schools. The most effective list is one that consists of schools located in the same area in which you are promoting. However, even if the list includes no schools within the prospect's area, it will still be very effective. If possible, include an entire sheet filled with the names and phone numbers of schools where you have performed in the last year or so. A long list implies that you have been very successful and have a solid reputation.

## Scheduling and booking information

Include a clearly defined section that provides all the information the prospect needs to contact you and book the program: who to call, when to call, the phone number, and what information to leave if they reach your message machine. Don't make the reader wade through the entire package looking for contact information.

## Technical considerations

In designing promotional packages for schools, keep in mind that the content, neatness, and organization of the package is far more important than glossy papers, colored inks, expensive logos and the like. With a limited budget for promotion, money is better spent on a large distribution of inexpensively produced packages than a limited distribution of glitzy ones. The trick is finding the point of diminished return on expensive production.

Colored inks really brighten up the promo, but more than double the printing expense and, in our experience, do not generate a measurable increase in response. If you are using a folder format, add color by using colored papers on the inner pieces; it's much less expensive than using colored inks.

Through the use of half-tones or screenings, photographs can be inexpensively included in a brochure or other promotional piece. Some artists prefer to have multiple copies made of their portrait photograph and include them separately with their promo packet. These do look nicer than screened photos; however, it is difficult to imagine that the expense is justified.

Particularly if you are printing on both sides of the paper, a slightly heavier paper (60 pound) produces a much nicer product for very little additional expense. Beyond this, I have not found expensive, fancy papers a good investment. We use nothing but standard bond papers.

Letterhead envelopes will make your promotion look more professional. For a long time we did not use them. Figuring that the envelope would be opened and discarded immediately, we wanted to spend our money on what was inside. Since we now have a larger budget for promotion and have found a great bargain on letterhead envelopes, we use them. I can't honestly say whether they make any difference in the return. If so, it's a minor one. If your budget is tight, and spending money on letterhead envelopes will cut into what you can spend on the promo inside the envelope, don't use them.

## How many pieces?

Depending on many factors, a promotion will typically generate from two to ten bookings for every hundred promo packets you send out. If you are booking a tour any distance away from your home base, send out more promo than you think necessary; it's far better to overspend a little on promotion than to get caught with too few bookings on a tour. If you do not get things booked tightly enough, road expenses (motels, gas, meals) will quickly consume your profits.

## When to mail the promo

Ideally, the promo should be mailed just prior to the time the schools begin scheduling their assembly programs. However, pinpointing this exact time is very difficult. Some schools do their scheduling in the spring, booking shows for the coming year. Others wait until late summer or until after school begins in the fall. Still others follow no pattern at all, booking an artist whenever they are struck by an attractive promotion, sometimes scheduling a show on a few days notice. Looking at the panel of excerpts from interviews with principals (page 58), you can see that most try to complete scheduling assemblies by the fall. However, promotions at other times of the year can be very effective. We have found early January to be an excellent time to promote, especially for booking spring dates.

Identifying poor times to promote is a little easier. Around Christmas is not a good time. Neither are the last days of the school year or the early summer months, when all attention is focused on ending the current year and beginning summer vacation. In summary, you do not want the promo to hit when it will be filed until a more *convenient* time. Chances are it will remain filed forever.

The specific dates you make yourself available to schools also affects the response to a promotion. We have found it much easier to book spring dates than fall dates. Perhaps this is because at the beginning of the school year and during the holiday season, the schools are involved in too many activities to consider adding assembly programs to the schedule.

When promoting to schools that will be sent a roster from an arts commission with which you are working, consider timing your promotion so it hits a few days after the roster, serving as a follow-up to the information they received from the commission. In any event, because some commissions have a fairly slow turn-around time, send your promotion at least two months in advance of the dates you want to book, in order to give the schools time to obtain and fill out applications for funding support.

## Mailing via bulk-mail

If you will be mailing large promotions (over 200 pieces) on a regular basis, consider getting a bulk mail permit. This will save you money on postage, especially if your packages weigh more than an ounce, since bulk mail pieces are allowed to weigh up to slightly more than 4 ounces before the per-piece rate goes up. The tradeoff is the extra work required to prepare bulk mail: the pieces must be sorted by zip code, bundled, and placed in mail sacks in accordance to strict postal regulations. Another tradeoff is that bulk mail goes third class, making it much more difficult to time exactly when the promo will hit. Delivery time ranges from a few days to over three weeks.

## Who to direct the promo to

It is impossible to know, from school to school, who actually books the assemblies. Possibilities include the principal, the PTA, a teacher designated as assembly coordinator, and the music teacher. In my experience, the majority of the time it's the principal who does the booking, and most of the rest of the time it's someone in the PTA. What I don't know is how often one of these people has had an influence over the other. Since postage is the largest portion of the promotional expense and the brochures are relatively inexpensive, we include two copies of the brochure in one envelope addressed to the school. The top line of the mail label is merely the name of the school—no indication of a person or job title. Printed along the bottom of the outer envelope is the following line: "Secretary: please open and distribute one copy each to the principal and PTA chairperson." This way, we're getting a package to a second person for only a few additional pennies. If you're mailing first class, this technique saves money only when the promotional package is light enough that the second package does not push the total weight over an ounce. (Two packages consisting of a brochure printed on 60 pound, 8½ x 11 paper and a cover letter, stuffed into one #10 envelope, just barely come in under one ounce.)

## The response pattern

The response curve of a promotion will vary depending on the time of year, whether or not the program ties into an upcoming calendar event, the effectiveness of the package, and other factors. As an example, after sending a January promotion to book a spring tour, we receive about half the total number of calls within ten days of the promotion's delivery. Most of the rest of the calls come in over the second ten days, with the remainder straggling in over the next several weeks.

## Follow-up promo

If you are booking a tour or block of dates and do not get enough response to fill up your schedule, consider designing a follow-up promotion. Surprisingly, the response to a follow-up is often greater than that generated by the original promotion. Include some sort of calendar that shows your current bookings and available dates (see Figure 4-2). Displaying your bookings in this manner not only makes you look successful, but the power of suggestion seems to generate bookings from schools in the same cities and districts as the ones shown scheduled on your calendar.

## How many shows can you schedule per day?

The amount of time it takes you to set up and tear down, the length of your program, the proximity of the schools, and the amount of stamina you have, will all affect the number of shows you can perform in a day. With a setup time of thirty minutes and a tear-down time of fifteen minutes, you should be able to perform at two locations during the morning. Because the afternoon is typically the shorter half of the school day, you'll have to tighten things up to have time for two shows in the afternoon.

When touring, some artists—trying to offset road expenses with high daily income—perform at four locations a day.

Program offerings are *Songs for a Bright Tomorrow* and *Folk Music in America*. You will find descriptions of the programs on the back panel. Each program is 40 minutes in length. Please refer to the schedule below to find an opening in your area (we can travel up to 120 miles between morning and afternoon locations in most cases).

March 31: AM: California Elementary School (West Covina)
PM: **OPEN**

April 1: AM: **OPEN**
PM: Gilcrest Elementary School (Napa)

April 2: AM: Providencia Elementary School (Burbank)
PM: **OPEN**

April 26: AM: Bronte Elementary School (Richmond)
PM: **OPEN**

April 27: AM: Coleman Elementary School (Orangeville)
PM: **OPEN**

April 28: AM: Evergreen Elementary School (Sacramento)
PM: **OPEN**

April 29: AM: Skyline Elementary School (Daly City)
PM: **OPEN**

May 3: AM: Page Elementary School (Santa Rosa)
PM: **OPEN**

May 6: AM: **OPEN**
PM: Durham Elementary School (Chico)

May 7: AM: Manzanita Elementary School (Redding)
PM: **OPEN**

Figure 4-2: An excerpt from a follow-up promotional piece. The listing of open dates in calendar format along with current bookings invokes the power of suggestion in filling up the schedule.

However, this is very taxing and not for the faint of heart. Be careful not to over commit yourself; your reputation and sanity will be at stake.

## PHONE WORK

### Prequalifying & follow-up phone calls

When promoting to a large number of schools, calling each school to determine whether or not the principal or other contact person is interested in receiving a promotional package is not practical. However, in cases where the number of schools is small, prequalifying calls are an option. In deciding whether or not to make prequalifying calls, keep in mind that, for each school, it will take several calls to actually connect with the right person—never request or expect prospects to return your call. The process is very time-consuming, and if the calls are long distance, costs will add up quickly. Furthermore, you must call these same prospects again after they have received the promotional package—with the time and effort expended thus far, it only makes sense to make a final attempt to get the booking.

Prequalifying and follow-up phone work requires a thick skin; over-worked secretaries and principals are often irritated by unsolicited calls. Most artists, considering promotion a necessary evil at best, quickly tire of the process. A wide distribution of low-cost, professional-looking promo packages will increase call-back response, reduce phone work, and make the act of promotion far more tolerable.

### Answering the phone

Be prepared to answer the phone in a professional manner. You'll be talking to school officials, and they are concerned not only about the quality of your program, but your professionalism as well. Your telephone manner will be their first clue. If

68

you are like many artists, your business phone and personal phone are one and the same. This makes professionalism a little trickier, particularly if you have a family or often host visitors. Make sure everyone is aware of the fact that you may have business calls coming in.

## Audience size

The maximum size audience for which you'd like to perform should be discussed with the contact person at the time the performance is booked. The number of students' energy you can keep channeled in a positive way depends on many factors, including your experience, the ways in which you are asking them to participate, and how well they need to see you. With rare exception, the number of students should not exceed 500. If you have a program with segments of audience participation that require space for significant movement, a program that is visual in nature, or if you lack experience performing for children, set your maximum audience size much lower.

## Audience age grouping

If you are presenting more than one show at the same school, you must decide how you want the student body divided. This should be discussed with the contact person during the initial conversation. Most performers prefer to have students divided by grade level, with kindergarten through third-grade students attending one show while fourth- through sixth-grade students attend the other. Usually, modifications are made to the program content, particularly NPC, in order to target the specific age group.

## Summary

Remember the following points when planning and executing a promotion to schools:

- Let the prospect know that you have an educational pro-

69

gram and possess the skills to effectively present it. Hammer this point in by stating the educational objective, including a list of schools where you have performed and letters of recommendation from principals, listing arts-in-education programs that sponsor you, and incorporating phrases throughout the promo that indicate your awareness of concepts such as audience engagement, audience management, and audience participation.

- Quality letters of recommendation are the most influential aspect of the promo package.

- Your money is better spent on large quantities of inexpensive, professional-looking promotional pieces than glitzy production.

- The two most effective times of the year for sending promotion are late summer/early fall and the first part of January.

- There is more demand for spring dates than fall dates.

- Promotion is best directed to principals, PTA chairpersons, music teachers, or all three.

If you have little or no experience performing in schools, it is impossible to include a long list of schools where you have performed, boast of various arts-in-education programs that sponsor you, and present endless quotes from letters of recommendation raving about your program and presentation skills. The following steps will help you acquire resources for your first promotion, build a strong reputation for both yourself and your program, and compete with established artists:

- after each trial performance of your program (see Chapter 3), ask for a letter of recommendation from the principal and evaluations from the teachers

- be open and responsive to criticism, record and critique your performances, and strive to make every presentation of the program superior to the previous one

- represent yourself as an organized and professional businessperson

- charge a fee that is highly competitive.

Success breeds success. Your reputation will build. Promotion and marketing will get easier and more profitable in time.

# CHAPTER 5
# How to Earn $3000 per Week Touring

To yield significant income, a tour must be tightly booked—four shows per day is the goal. In working toward this goal do the following:

- plan tours only in highly populated areas

- execute a three-step promotional campaign

- offer the schools a variety of dates and programs from which to choose

- charge a competitive fee

- develop the ability to set up, perform the program, sell recordings and publications, tear down, and get back on the road in a highly efficient and expeditious manner.

**Geographical considerations**

Plan to visit a number of highly populated areas, lodge in the center of the area, and perform in schools within a seventy- to ninety-mile radius. After staying in the area for a number of days, plan to move on to the next highly populated area. On the way back home, you'll stop in these same areas again. By returning to each area, you'll be able to offer the schools a wider variety of dates from which to choose. This flexibility will increase the number of bookings obtained.

The following is a description of a five-week tour route my duo has taken many times: We begin in the Seattle area on a Monday, stay for three days, and finish the week in Portland. Over the weekend we travel to Sacramento. After spending Monday and Tuesday of the second week in Sacramento, we move on to the Bay Area—Oakland, San Francisco, and surrounding communities. Over the next weekend we travel to Los Angeles and spend the third week there. The next weekend begins the trip back. The fourth week is spent in the Bay Area and Sacramento, and the final week in Portland and Seattle.

Do not attempt to tour small towns in lightly populated areas. Small towns tend to have small schools with small budgets; there is little money for funding special presentations. Because towns in lightly populated areas are spread out, even if you do get a few bookings, the increased driving time usually makes it impossible to get from a booking in one town to a booking in the next town the same morning or afternoon. It's best to skip small towns even when you'll be driving through them on your way to a populated area. (You'll notice in the above description of our five-week tour route that we skip even moderately populated areas like the Springfield/Eugene area in Oregon and Redding, California.)

**Calendar considerations**

The best months to plan an extensive tour are January through May. Before scheduling tours in the period from mid-March to mid-April, contact major districts in each area to find out when spring break is scheduled; most schools in the area will adhere to the same vacation schedule. Kick off the promotional campaign for a January or February tour in November and then dodge the holiday vacation schedule as the campaign proceeds. (Because of the manner in which the winter holiday season interferes with the execution of the promotional campaign, tours in January and February are more difficult to book than spring tours.) Wait until early January before promoting tours scheduled for spring.

## A three-step promotional plan

The first step in booking a tour is to send a promo packet to every school in the areas you will be visiting. Include a schedule indicating when you will be in each of the areas.

After three to four weeks, the tour should be partially booked. The second step is to mail a *fill-in-the-gaps* promotion. In the packets, include a calendar listing the schools where you are currently booked. Be sure to include the city in which each school is located as well as highlighting the available dates. (See Chapter 4 for more details on setting up the calendar.)

After another three or four weeks, the fill in the-gaps promotion will have run its course. Ideally, this will book the tour to near capacity. Then, two to three weeks before the tour, wherever there is an opening in the schedule, send ten nearby schools a third promo packet with a personalized letter informing the principal that you will be in their immediate area (provide the name and district of the school at which you're booked), and offer the program at half price when they schedule a program the specific day and time you have open. Settling for half price hurts a little, but it's better to accept a reduced fee than allow a slot to remain unbooked. Since you'll be in the area anyway, there will be no additional costs incurred in doing the discounted show—the income will be pure profit.

## Multiple program offerings

Offering more than one program increases your chances of a full schedule. If one or more of the programs tie into the late winter/spring calendar, you will increase the response even further. Potential calendar tie-ins include Martin Luther King Day, Black History Month, Lincoln's Birthday, President's Day,

Washington's Birthday, Earth Day, May Day, Cinco de Mayo, and Memorial Day.

## Efficiency

How tightly you can book the tour—and then stay on schedule—will depend on your efficiency in many areas. The speed in which you can set up and tear down is a crucial factor. A few minutes difference in the time required will determine whether or not you're able to visit two schools in the same morning or afternoon. Reduce, down-size, and combine your equipment as much as possible (see Chapter 8 for suggestions in this area). Get your gear on wheels. For example, I installed dolly wheels on the underside of my guitar case, put a handle on the end of the case, and attached a belt, allowing my partner's guitar to be strapped on top. Additionally, I custom built a dolly for our sound system—everything fits on in one load. After unloading the car, my partner goes ahead of me with the guitars, pulls open doors with her free hand to let me through with the equipment dolly, and then wheels the guitars in behind her. By reducing the process to one trip, wheeling gear instead of carrying it, and eliminating the need to prop doors open, we save several precious minutes. The savings are doubled after we make the trip back to the car following tear-down.

During the actual setup, time will be saved and errors reduced by having a predetermined series of tasks for each member of the ensemble to perform, keeping the need for communication to a minimum, and having all connections, jacks, and plugs clearly labeled.

Get the show started on time. The fact that you are on schedule is no guarantee that the program will begin at the appointed time. All too often—without your gentle but firm guidance—students will not even begin arriving until show time. Here is a recipe for getting the school to start the program on time:

- Include in the material you send to the school seven days before the performance (see Chapter 6) a reminder that, due to a tight schedule, the show must start on time to allow for a full-length program.

- Upon checking in at the office, verbally reinforce the need to start on time.

- If students have not begun arriving ten minutes before show time, return to the office and inform the secretary that you have finished setting up and are ready for students to begin arriving.

- If you have not been introduced by the time the show is scheduled to start, stand up, begin strapping on instruments, and move toward the microphones—look like you are ready to go. This will often cause the audience to hush and the emcee to begin making her way to the microphone

If you have recordings or publications to sell following the program, develop a credit system that makes it quick and easy for teachers to purchase them (see Chapter 10 for details). Explain how the system works in a carefully crafted script just before the end of the show. Continually modify this script until it gets the idea across in the clearest possible way, eliminating the need to make further explanations to individual teachers as they come forward after the program. In addition, design a hand-out that lists the contents of recordings or publications and provides prices, allowing interested teachers to readily see what you have to offer. This will prevent you from being tied up over and over answering the same questions, as well as eliminate the need to keep track of merchandise you have handed out for teachers to examine.

At first, you may think that conducting everything in such a highly-prepared, military-like fashion will be incredibly stressful. Actually the opposite is true. Once these procedures become automated, they reduce stress by preventing mistakes, saving time, and increasing profitability.

## Getting to $3000 per week

Based on a regular fee of $250 per show, a second-show fee of $100, and a half-price, special fee of $125 for a school that takes a specific time slot, let's take a look at the range of daily-income possibilities in a fully booked tour. The highest income would occur when two full-price, single shows are scheduled in the morning and two more in the afternoon—a total of $1000. The low end of the spectrum would occur when a single show is scheduled in the morning at full price, a half-price show is squeezed in before lunch, and a single, full-price show is scheduled in the afternoon—a total of $500. There are many combinations in between these two extremes that will yield $600 to $900. Even considering cancellations and slots that remain unbooked, $3000 per week is an attainable goal.

◆ ◆ ◆

Planning, promoting, and executing an extensive tour of schools is not something to be undertaken without considerable experience. The costs of touring are significant; if a tour is sparsely booked, you may actually lose money. Build a strong reputation, develop a promotional packet that wins four or five bookings out of every hundred sent, and get your systems down to a science before considering your first tour.

77

# CHAPTER 6
# Paperwork

Once a program is booked, a well-orchestrated flow of paper-work will prevent awkward misunderstandings with the school over scheduling and payment details and put you in control of a number of variables that can affect the outcome of your presentation.

**Timing**

Proper timing will maximize the effectiveness of post-booking paperwork. Don't simply stuff everything into one big envelope and send it all at the same time. Such an approach will lead to many matters being overlooked by the principal or contact person. Send paperwork on a need-to-do basis, following the schedule below:

- immediately following the booking, send a letter of confirmation and invoice

- six weeks from the performance, send publicity materials and preparation materials

- seven days from the performance, send a list of reminders and a second copy of preparation materials.

## Letter of confirmation

Design a contract or letter of confirmation (see Figure 6-1) that reflects your understanding of verbal agreements made in the following areas:

- date(s) and time(s) of performance(s)

- the length of the program

- fee information: the total amount, when you expect to be paid, to whom to make the check payable

- your social security number

- state business license number (Many school districts have regulations prohibiting them from contracting with individuals or businesses who do not have a state license number.)

- federal ID number (Some districts require this in order to treat you as a contractor rather than an employee, allowing them to pay you without deducting taxes from your check. Contact your local IRS office for information on obtaining a federal ID number.)

- setup and equipment requirements

- the deadline after which significant changes to the agreement cannot be made.

Also, confirm any other verbal arrangements you have made, such as the grade levels of students you'll be performing for, maximum (or minimum) number of students in the audience, or other factors that will affect the success of the program.

It is important to remember that the letter of confirmation is just what the title implies: a confirmation of matters previously agreed upon. Don't include any surprises. If there are matters you neglected to discuss with the contact person during the booking process, call the contact person back and discuss these items *before* sending the letter of confirmation.

**Confirmation of date, time, and financial arrangement**

Assembly Coordinator:
School:
Address:

Name of program:
Date of program:
Time of program:
Length of program:
Fee:

Please be prepared to make payment as indicated:

[ ] on the date of the performance
[ ] via purchase order or school contract (Payment expected
  within 30 days of the performance.)

<u>Sound System</u>
Dave & Cindy are equipped with a professional sound system.
Please do not set up the school sound system. To allow for
setup, please make arrangements to have the performance room
cleared of activity 20 minutes in advance of the performance
time.

<u>Preparation Materials</u>
In advance of the scheduled program date, you will receive a
preparation packet which includes a song sheet, a study guide,
fliers, and information for the school newsletter.

Figure 6-1: A letter of confirmation form sent to the schools within
five days of booking the performance.

You may send a contract rather than a letter of confirmation. The primary difference between a contract and a letter of confirmation is that the latter does not have to be signed and returned. Because we seldom have problems with schools canceling performances on short notice or failing to live up to verbal agreements, and because keeping track of who has returned their contract and who needs to be reminded to do so is tedious and time consuming, we prefer the letter of confirmation.

## Invoice

Many schools will require an invoice (see Figure 6-2) in order to make payment. Create a form that states the following: the amount you are billing, the name of the program the billing is for, the date and time the program is to be performed, and the date by which you expect payment. Also, include your federal ID number, state license number, social security number, address, and phone number.

## Study guides

Study guides should be sent six weeks in advance of the day of the performance. (See Chapter 3 for details on developing study guides.)

## Fliers

Fliers or posters are definitely optional. However, I believe fliers with the artists' picture and where-and-when information regarding the performance help build student anticipation: when you arrive there is a sense of excitement—students know who you are and why you're there. Fliers can be inexpensively produced on 8½ x 11, twenty-pound bond paper. Send each school you book four or five of them.

# INVOICE

Contact person:
School:
School address:
Program name:
Fee:
Date service provided:
Provided by: Dave & Cindy
Tax classification: sole proprietorship
Federal ID number: xx-xxxxxxx
Washington State UBI: x xxx xxx xxx
Social security number: xxx xxx xxxx

Payment is expected on the date of performance unless a purchase order is sent to DAVE & CINDY at the address above. Payment through purchase order is expected within 30 days following the performance.

Please make check payable to Dave & Cindy.

Mail purchase orders to:

Dave & Cindy
P.O. Box 1407
Orient, WA 99160

Thank you.

Figure 6-2: An invoice sent with the letter of confirmation within five days of booking the performance

### NEWSLETTER/BULLETIN INFORMATION

**Dave & Cindy,** a professional guitar and vocal duo specializing in entertaining, educational assembly programs, will be performing for the students of _____ Elementary School on _____(date) at _____(time).

Their program, *Folk Music in America,* provides a fun and educational look at Americans as reflected in our heritage of folk songs. Through the songs, students will gain insights into American attitudes and feelings, past and present, about their country, their work, their play, their hopes, and their dreams. Songs include *Goober Peas, A Place in the Choir, Puff the Magic Dragon, This Land is Your Land,* and other favorites. Students participate throughout the program by singing along, signing American Sign Language, and clapping rhythms.

*Folk Music in America* was originally created for the Washington State Arts Commission's Cultural Enrichment Program and has been presented in hundreds of schools in Washington, Oregon, California, and Idaho.

Figure 6-3: A double-spaced press release for the school's newsletter and bulletin.

## Newsletter/bulletin information

Send a simple press release (see Figure 6-3) the school can use to print information regarding the program in bulletins and newsletters. Include the following:

- when and where the performance will take place

- the nature of your program—the art form, size of the ensemble, etc.

- what students will learn during the program

- how students will be involved in the program

- titles or concise descriptions of key performance pieces.

## Cover letter

Create a cover letter explaining to the principal or contact person what action to take regarding each of the enclosures in the packet of preparation materials. (See Figure 6-4.)

## Last-minute reminders

Seven to ten days in advance of your performance, send a list of reminders reviewing agreements about your performance (see Figure 6-5). Include reminders about the following:

- the length of time you need to set up

- your need for the performance space to be free of activity during setup

- special equipment or dressing room needs

- student preparation

- turning off school bells in the performance facility

- payment detail

- seating requirements.

TO:      Assembly Coordinator
FROM: Dave & Cindy
RE:       Assembly Program

Enclosed are fliers, newsletter/bulletin information, study guides, and refrains to key songs in the program, *Folk Music in America*. Please use these materials to prepare for the assembly as indicated below:

**Fliers**: Please display the fliers in prominent places (office, lunchroom, hallway bulletin boards).

**Bulletin Information**: This information may be used verbatim or in an edited version for the school newsletter, bulletin, or other media.

**Song Refrains**: Audience participation is emphasized throughout the program. Student exposure to the enclosed refrains will greatly enhance student involvement in the program and increase student retention of the educational content of the program. Please distribute copies to the music teacher and/or classroom teachers as appropriate.

**Study Guides**: Classroom discussion of the subject matter presented in the program will greatly facilitate student comprehension of the educational content of the program. Please provide a copy of the study guides to each of the classroom teachers.

We thank you for your efforts in preparing students for the upcoming assembly program.

Figure 6-4: Cover letter to accompany the packet of preparation materials sent to the school six weeks before the performance.

Thank you for inviting us to present *Folk Music in America* for your students. The following reminders will help ensure an enjoyable assembly experience for both the audience and the performers.

1. WE PROVIDE OUR OWN SOUND SYSTEM. Please arrange to have the performance area cleared of student activity 20 minutes in advance of the scheduled start time so we may set up our sound system. If the performance is to be held in the gym, please advise the PE teacher of our need for a quiet, activity-free environment beginning 20 minutes before show time. The provision of the following will be greatly appreciated:

   * two small tables or flat-top desks
   * an extension cord (if nearest outlet is more than 20 feet away)

2. PLEASE FAMILIARIZE STUDENTS WITH THE SONGS on the enclosed song sheet. Music teachers were sent the song sheet several weeks ago. Please request that they run through the refrains with students. Even minimal exposure to the music in advance of the program greatly enhances audience participation.

3. IT IS CRITICAL THAT THE ASSEMBLY START ON TIME to allow for a full program. Due to a tight schedule we must end the program 40 minutes after the **scheduled** start time.

4. PLEASE HAVE SCHOOL BELLS TURNED OFF in the performance facility during the assembly if your bell system allows.

5. PLEASE ARRANGE FOR PAYMENT on the day of the performance unless other arrangements have been agreed upon.

6. SEATING ARRANGEMENT. We prefer not to use a stage. Typically, we stand on the floor about 6 feet out from the wall. The first row of students should be seated on the floor (no chairs please) approximately 6 feet back from our microphone stands. The youngest students should be in the first row; the oldest students should comprise the last row. **Please arrange for chairs to be set up for teachers** along the outside aisles. **Please avoid seating students on bleachers** except where floor seating is impossible.

Figure 6-5: A list of reminders sent to the school ten days before the scheduled program.

The reminder sheet will greatly reduce the likelihood of problems and complications on the day of the performance, making the event a positive one for all concerned. In some cases, the sheet will prompt calls from principals or contact persons who realize after reading it that for some reason they will not be able to live up to an earlier agreement in one or more of the areas addressed. Knowing this in advance will provide an opportunity to work out an alternative arrangement several days—rather than several minutes—before the performance.

## Seating configuration

Let the principal or contact person know how you want the audience to be seated. This can be done in description form on the reminder sheet or by means of a seating chart.

Most principals have a standard seating arrangement they follow anytime the entire student body is assembled for a presentation. The most common arrangement is for each class to form a row extending all the way from one side of the facility to the other. Generally, the youngest students are seated in the front and the oldest in the back. Another arrangement, though far less common, is seating each class in a block approximately as deep as it is wide. Getting principals to agree to seat the students in a manner that strays very far from the standard is difficult. However, they are usually willing to make minor modifications regarding whether the rows are curved or straight, where aisles are formed, whether or not the students are in chairs, and the amount of space between the rows. In articulating your seating requirements, the following are key considerations:

- If it is important that the audience be able to see anything below your shoulders and you will not be using a stage, children will be able to see much better if they are seated on the floor rather than in chairs. This arrangement increases the sight angle between the students and performers, making it easier for children to see over the tops of the heads in front of them. Chairs also take up more space, require more time for seating, cause the audience to be spread out further, and have a great potential for making noise during the program.

● Because of differences in height, younger children should not be sitting behind older ones. Surprisingly, sometimes school administrators overlook this fact. To be on the safe side, request that the youngest students be in front and the oldest students in back.

● If you like to mingle with the audience or plan to have students come forward to participate with the artists, a center aisle is a must.

● If students need more space for group participation than knee-to-knee, cross-legged sitting allows, specify the amount of space required. Describe the specification in a way that, when conveyed by their teacher, small children will readily understand: "Students will need enough space to fully extend their arms to the side without touching the hand of the person next to them," rather than, "Students need to be seated five feet apart from one another."

● Specify whether you want your audience seated in straight rows or a semicircle (curved-row arrangement). Curved rows cut down the amount of space between performer and audience, but can create visibility problems since the front rows will wrap around to the side of the artists' performing area. This arrangement is not desirable for artists who remain stationary, facing forward during the performance. If you move from one side of the semicircle to the other during the performance, engaging the students off to the sides, the curved-row format works well. If you decide on this arrangement, be prepared to assist students is getting situated—they often have difficulty understanding the concept of curved rows.

Avoid having the kids seated on bleachers. The temptation for students to stomp their feet is strong. Once started, this activity spreads quickly and is hard to stop. Because it is difficult for teachers to see what students' feet are doing, it's easy for students who are stomping on the bleachers to avoid detection.

## Student assistance

If you need student help in unloading, setting up, tearing down, and reloading your equipment, let the principal or contact person know in advance so they can make the necessary arrangements. Have students handle the lighter, sturdier gear. Leave heavy equipment and fragile instruments to members of the ensemble.

## Directions to the school

Even if you are an expert with maps, get directions to the school. There is no worse feeling than successfully navigating yourself through rush hour traffic to the wrong location. Always reconcile directions with a map and vice versa.

## Summary

Post-booking paperwork includes the following:

● letter of confirmation or contract

● invoice

● study guides

● fliers

● press release

● reminder sheet

● seating chart.

Send the above paperwork in three separate mailings as indicated below:

Immediately following booking: letter of confirmation/contract and invoice

Six weeks before program: study guides, fliers, press release

Seven days before program: reminder sheet, second copy of study guides, seating chart.

# CHAPTER 7
# Pre-show Concerns

*Be on time, be prepared, make sure all your stuff works, determine who the authority figure in the school is so you have some assistance with crowd control and management, start the assembly when you say you're going to start it and end it when you say you're going to end it.* - Tim O'Brien, Principal, Issaquah ES, Issaquah WA

## First things first

Check in at the office upon arriving at the school to announce your arrival, take care of any paperwork details, and find out where to set up for the performance.

Ask someone in the office to escort you to the performance facility. This will prevent a number of undesirable developments: First, you will not lose precious setup time looking for the facility. Secondly, you will not have to walk back to the office to get a key after finding the door to the facility locked. And most importantly, you will have a staff member with some authority to tell the P.E. teacher, who is almost always out of the school's communication loop, that the playing of *slaughter ball* will not be compatible with your setup needs.

## Use of the stage

There are both pros and cons to using the stage. On the one hand, being on stage makes it easier for students to see, particularly if the content of your program requires the audience to see anything less than three feet above floor level. The stage also allows more flexibility in setting up. On the other hand, being on the stage can make it difficult to mingle with the audience or bring volunteers forward during segments of audience participation. It also makes the audience-artist relationship less intimate.

Often you will have no choice regarding the use of the stage. In many cases, there will not be one. Other times you'll have to use the stage in order to allow room for audience seating. Plan to be very flexible in this area.

### Audience traffic flow

Before you begin setting up your equipment, determine where the students will be entering and exiting; keep these routes clear of cables, speakers, and other gear. In addition, take into consideration the location of restrooms, drinking fountains, and other popular destinations.

### Power outlets

Find out right away if there are functional outlets within range of your extension cord. (To keep equipment weight down, many artists carry only a twenty-foot cord, which is sufficient in most situations). Also, if you have equipment that draws high current levels, make sure the outlets are capable of supplying the required current without blowing fuses; if not, you will need additional extension cords to spread the power demand over several outlets. (I've seen an electric drill used to test the fuse-blowing potential of outlets when equipment power demand was heavy.) If you discover problems with outlets or need extension cords, get word back to the office immediately—it may take awhile before help arrives. We learned this the hard way: After setting up one morning, we discovered the outlets didn't work. We immediately informed the office of the situation, but it took several minutes for the custodian to arrive. After a long and fruitless search, he was unable to find the fuse switch. With only minutes remaining before show time, he advised us to set up at the other end of the gym, where the outlets were working. By the time we had accomplished the second setup, the students were already arriving, leaving no time for instrument tuning, sound checks, or anything else.

For self-evident reasons, avoid the use of outlets that are within reach of students.

## Sound check

Before you conduct a sound check, close the doors to the performance facility—teachers down the hall will appreciate the consideration.

Pay special attention to volume. Many times there will be students in the audience who are very sensitive to high decibel levels; others may have been exposed to sound-system abuse. Since there's a tendency to speak and play louder during the actual performance than during the sound check, use no more volume than that required to be comfortably heard in the back of the room. A good policy is to begin the show with the volume a little on the soft side, a few minutes into the program ask teachers in the back of the room if the sound level is adequate, and then increase the volume if necessary.

If you see students with their hands over their ears while you are performing, it may not necessarily be an indication that the volume is too high. Often students will *play* with sound by cupping their hands over their ears or pushing their hands back and forth against their ears to impose special effects on the sound. Observing their facial expressions is the key to determining whether they are playing around or in pain. If you see a number of students with their hands over their ears and strained looks on their faces, the sound is definitely too loud—turn it down immediately!

## Time restraints

Because programs invariably start late, ask the principal if there is a time by which you must end the program in order to keep the school on schedule—many times there will be a lunch hour, recess, or student dismissal immediately after the time your show is scheduled to conclude. If so, knowing the cut-off time in advance will allow you to be selective in deciding what program content to omit if the program is running late. This is much preferable to abruptly ending the program after deciphering a *cut* signal from the principal.

## School announcements or activities

Often principals will want to make announcements about school activities or make various presentations, taking advantage of the fact that the entire student body is assembled. Try to be flexible, but watch out for yourself at the same time. Suggest they do these things after—rather than before—the program. Having students seated on the floor or in hard chairs for ten or fifteen minutes before you get started puts you at an immediate disadvantage.

## As the students come in

Whether or not the audience gets seated in accordance with your seating chart (which you sent to the schools earlier) is largely up to you. If you leave the seating to chance, you may wind up with a huge gap in the middle of the room, a thirty-foot space between the stage and the front row, or the absence of a center aisle. The youngest students usually arrive first. Working with their teachers, guide the children into position, forming the first row the desired distance from the stage or performing area. Once the front row is established, the rest of the classes will fill in behind. It's much easier to get students seated correctly from the start than to try to adjust the entire student body later.

As the students continue to file in, you will get a sense of the audience's personality. With a little experience, you will know when to make minor adjustments to the program content. With some audiences, you'll be able to loosen up and ad lib a little, going out on a limb or two. With others, the best course of action is to run a tight ship and stick to a proven script.

## Introduction

The manner in which you are introduced can have an immediate effect on the show. It's important that the person who introduces you sets an appropriate tone for the program. There is only one way to make sure this happens: have the introduction preprinted on a 3x5 index card and ask the person officiating to use it. Most people are overjoyed that they don't have to improvise. Set up a microphone especially for them to use. Direct students that will be making announcements or leading flag salutes to use this microphone as well. This will reduce the possibility of damage to your expensive microphones and spare you direct exposure to any contagious illnesses they may have. (This may appear a little neurotic until the first time you find yourself reattaching the head of your new microphone with duct tape or canceling a series of performances due to illness.)

As the introduction is read from one place to the next, notice if any of the words or phrases cause an undesirable reaction. For example, in the introduction to one of our programs, the word *duo* used to occur. At least half the people reading the introduction would stop and conduct a question-and-answer session with the students as to what *duo* means. This would sometimes go on for an eternity. We have since deleted this word, but somehow the phrase *together for twelve years* slipped in. Twelve years is greater than the age of most people in our audience. This fact did not escape them. While the kids were oohing and aahing over how long twelve years was, you could see the wheels spinning in the heads of the faculty: "Gee, I wonder how old that makes them...how old do you suppose they were when they got started." After a few minutes, order would be restored, and the introduction would proceed. Needless to say, we have since deleted that phrase.

## Summary

After you have arrived at the school, you will need to do the following:

- check in at the office

- find the performance area and determine whether or not to use the stage

- test the electrical outlets

- set up, taking into consideration audience traffic flow

- conduct a sound check

- get a preprinted introduction to the appropriate person and familiarize them with the emcee microphone

- determine if there is a time by which you *must* end the program

- assist with student seating.

# CHAPTER 8
# Sound Reinforcement

Most of the time, a school performance is presented in the multipurpose room (MPR) or gymnasium. Acoustics in these rooms range from bad to worse. Often there is no sound system. Even when available, school sound systems are usually totally inadequate for performing-arts programs. Providing and effectively operating your own sound system are mandatory for high-quality sound reinforcement.

## How a gymnasium affects amplified sound

A gym or MPR sounds the way it does largely because the room's acoustics significantly amplify lower and mid-range frequencies, severely reducing intelligibility and clarity. Voices sound *muddy* and lack diction. Musical instruments, when amplified in a gym or MPR, are robbed of clarity, sparkle, and crispness. The lower notes of stringed instruments will sound *boomy*, while midrange notes may be harsh and out of balance.

An equalizer is the key to solving the acoustical problems inherent in a gym or MPR. In order for an artist's words to be clearly understood and instruments to be faithfully reproduced, cutting the frequencies ranging from 160 hz. to 2 khz. in the signal sent to the amplifier is required. Cutting these frequencies by a full twelve decibels is typical. In some cases

97

(particularly when working close-up to microphones, which aggravates the frequency-distortion problem), running the modified signal through the second channel of the equalizer is necessary to reduce these frequencies even further. In most gyms and MPRs, amplified sound will also benefit from a boost of 6 to 8 decibels in the high-frequency range (10 to 16 khz.). Using an equalizer in this manner eliminates *boominess* and adds sparkle, significantly improving the clarity and intelligibility of the sound.

## CONSIDERATIONS IN PURCHASING A SOUND SYSTEM

Minimum equipment requirements for a school performance are a professional-quality microphone, mixer, equalizer, amplifier, and speaker system. In addition to their ability to accurately and cleanly reproduce sound, an important factor in each of these components is their weight and size, which will affect the ease and speed in which your system can be set up. When on tour, the amount of setup time required will affect how many performances you can do in a day. While lightweight, compact equipment costs more, it quickly pays for itself through the extra shows it allows you to squeeze into the schedule.

### Microphones

A professional-quality microphone of the *dynamic* variety is the best bet for the school environment. Dynamic microphones are relatively inexpensive and capable of surviving a six-foot drop to the floor. A tight, unidirectional pick-up pattern will reduce feedback problems inherent in the large, concrete-constructed rooms in which you will often find yourself performing. Fitting the microphone with a wind screen permitting you to work very close to it will also help reduce feedback problems by allowing you to keep the microphone pre-amp setting relatively low.

## Mixer

Any professional-quality mixer will suffice for the school environment. However, mixers that have a tunable mid-range EQ section on each channel, allowing the operator to select both frequency and bandwidth, provide additional assistance in dealing with mid-range frequency boost—adjustments can be made to individual channels before the signal moves on to the main equalizer.

## Equalizer

An equalizer, for reasons discussed above, is a critical component in your system. A graphic equalizer is the easiest to use: as the name implies, it allows the user to *see*, in terms of frequency response, the effect the equalizer is having on the sound. Nearly all graphic equalizers are stereo, offering a second channel for further shaping of the frequency response when drastic measures are required.

## Amplifier

You will not need a particularly powerful amplifier; in most gyms and multipurpose rooms, sound does not need to be amplified as much as it needs to be shaped in terms of frequency response. A 100-watt amplifier should provide enough power. We uses a 60-watt amp. The only situations in which we were left wishing for a little more power were outdoor performances.

Amps represent the largest chunk of weight among a sound system's electronic components. However, there are currently amplifiers on the market that are quite light. We recently replaced our ten-year-old amp, measuring 30"x10"x12" and weighing 30 pounds, with a single-space, rack-mountable unit weighing ten pounds.

## Powered mixers

You may wish to consider a powered mixer. These units combine a mixer, amplifier, and often an equalizer in the same cabinet. Advantages include a lower price than the components cost separately, reduced weight and size since the components share the same cabinet, and faster, easier setup since these components are permanently interconnected. The main disadvantage is that powered mixers do not allow much flexibility in tailoring a sound system to your specific needs. You may need certain inputs, outputs, and controls that are not available on many powered mixers.

## Speakers

Speaker systems with a separate high-end transducer are mandatory for providing a clear, crisp sound. The high-frequency transducer should have a wide-dispersion cone. Avoid the *piezo* type of transducers; they do not have the capability to project the high frequencies to the back of a large MPR or gymnasium.

Look for speaker systems with lightweight cabinets, or have cabinets custom built. Most cabinets are made of extremely heavy pressboard, representing a major portion of the overall weight. (Our speaker systems originally weighed fifty pounds. Recently I reduced them to thirty-two pounds by designing and making new cabinets out of one-quarter-inch plywood.) Lightweight cabinets usually cost more because they must be made out of high-quality materials in order to be durable, but they are well worth the expense if you can afford them.

Speaker stands should be light weight, sturdy, and easy to set up and take down. We like the aluminum tripod kind the best.

## Pre-wiring

Perhaps the most time-consuming and error-prone aspect of setting up a sound system is connecting cables from one component to the other. Choosing light, compact components, packaging them together in a single cabinet, and pre-connecting the components greatly reduces setup time. In our system, the amplifier and equalizer are mounted in a rack directly beneath the mixer. The power cords have been shortened to reduce weight and are all plugged into a six-way power strip. All connections between the components are made with custom-length cables. The four microphone cables are bound together, allowing all four of them to be simultaneously unwound and routed.

◆ ◆ ◆

## Summary

The acoustical environment of the average school gymnasium or MPR provides a major challenge to high-quality sound reinforcement. The primary problem is lower and midrange frequency distortion that hampers the clarity and intelligibility of sound. Because schools typically have sound systems inadequate to the needs of a performing-arts presentation, having your own system is mandatory. An equalizer is required to effectively deal with the frequency distortion that occurs in a gym or MPR.

For touring artists, lightweight, compact systems quickly pay for themselves by reducing setup time, thus allowing more performances to be scheduled in the course of a day. Further reductions in setup time can be achieved by combining system components in a single cabinet, pre-connecting components, and binding together microphone cables.

# CHAPTER 9
# Program Presentation

The success of a school assembly performance is largely dependent on the artists' presentation skills. Effective presentation brings about a number of desirable results: appropriate audience behavior, enthusiastic audience participation, and high student retention of the program's educational content. Conversely, ineffective presentation leads to an inattentive, bored audience, dooming even the best-designed programs to mediocrity or failure.

## Setting a tone

*The initial several minutes are critical. You're like a substitute teacher coming in. You've got to make that first impression a good one. Avoid trying to become buddies with your audience. Don't ask questions of the audience like, "Well, did any of you see the TV show last night about such and such?...did you like it?" Now the kids are already all stirred up over two simple little questions you asked; they have no choice but to respond in a way that takes the direction way off kilter and creates an atmosphere where kids are shouting out answers, and you're already beginning to loose control.* - Cory Crawford, Principal, Fruitland ES, Puyallup WA

Regardless of your program's content, you must set an educational tone in the first few minutes of the program, establishing yourself not only as an educator, but the person in charge of the event as well. What you say, and how you say it, will affect your ability to manage the audience from this point on. As all classroom teachers will tell you, it's best to set a more serious tone to begin with and then loosen up later; trying to clamp down after beginning with an anything-goes attitude is next to impossible. Following are some things to remember in setting an educational tone:

- Do not ask questions of the audience that prompt students to call out answers without raising their hands.

- Do not address the audience until the room is absolutely quiet. Never talk over the top of audience chatter. Unfortunately, you will sometimes be introduced by a person who does not aspire to this standard. This makes your job more difficult, but not impossible. If the room starts out noisy, move up to the microphone as though you were about to begin speaking but decided not to, backing away from the microphone again: let your body language indicate that something is not right—that you can't begin yet.

- If students begin to talk while you are speaking, stop mid-sentence and wait until they are quiet again. If they do not quiet down after a few seconds, say something indicating that you will not go on until there is no talking; for example, you might say, "I'm going to wait for just a moment before going on because I hear some students talking and I know that makes it hard for the students next to them to hear."

- Convey to the audience, directly or indirectly, that the program will be educational as well as entertaining.

It's important to maintain a positive attitude when setting the desired tone. Don't appear frustrated or critical of the students' behavior if it falls short of the standard; simply convey, without passing judgment, that the behavior just won't work for this situation.

### Setting audience expectations

*To start each expectation with the word "don't" is going to be a real downer. But "here's when you can do this" and "here's when you can do that" will clearly communicate to the kids when to participate, when to listen, and what their behavior needs to be like.* - Brian Fox, Principal, Karshner ES, Puyallup WA

Somewhere in the first five minutes of the program, let the audience know what is expected of them. Since all programs are not alike, what's appropriate for one program may be inappropriate for another. The kids will not know what is appropriate for *your* program unless you tell them. For example, in our programs, after we have made a few introductory remarks, I let the audience know what we expect of them by saying the following:

Everywhere we have been on our tour, we have had excellent audiences. I can tell already that you are going to be a great audience for us this afternoon. But being a good audience can mean a lot of different things depending on what the program is like. So we thought it would be a good idea to let you know what we think would make a good audience for *our* program. That would be an audience that sings along when they hear a song they know or whenever we're teaching a song; listens very carefully when they are not singing; knows the best way to show appreciation after songs is by using only their hands to applaud—we wouldn't want to use whistling or shouting for this program; and most importantly, understands how important it is that we not have any talking during the program.

These are some of the things you can think about in terms of being a great audience for us.

Spelling out expectations also assists the teachers in evaluating the appropriateness of their students' behavior. This is not to say that they will necessarily do something about students whose behavior fails to meet the expectations, but it greatly increases the odds.

## Your manner of speech

Always target your manner of speech to the older students in the audience. Fifth- and sixth-grade students sometimes arrive at the assembly already suspecting that the program is beneath them; speaking in an overly animated way or in any other manner typical of speaking to very young children will alienate them immediately. Speak in an enthusiastic manner, but make sure the enthusiasm is genuine; contrived or phony enthusiasm is worse than none at all.

## Pacing

A quick pace is essential. Begin the next piece or activity before the applause from the previous piece has faded. Any gaps in the program, no matter how small, will contribute to a break-down in audience focus. In preventing such gaps, the use of cue cards is strongly recommended. My partner and I lay these out on the floor in front of us to keep ourselves continually informed of the next song or activity, whose turn it is to intro-duce the segment, what key the next song is in, what fret to place the capo on, etc.

## Inspiring group participation.

When calling for audience participation, have someone in your ensemble demonstrate whatever it is you're asking the students to do—provide the students with an example to follow.

This can be difficult if you are a solo act. For example, let's say you want the kids to use American Sign Language while you sing and play the guitar. It's impossible to both play the guitar and demonstrate the signs. You could, however, teach the signs to the audience first, watch for a student that catches on quickly, and then invite that student to come up and lead the group while you sing and play. (Pick the oldest, *coolest* looking student. They will inspire participation from the rest of the audience.)

With the first participation activity, allow some time for students to get comfortable with the idea of becoming involved in the program. For example, in our programs, we encourage students to sing along on many song refrains. On the first sing-along, I tell the audience I want them to start off nice and easy—about one-quarter volume. This is where they would start anyway, but because I tell them I *want* them to sing softly, it changes the dynamics. Instead of having a sense of failure as a result of singing softly, the students have a sense of success because singing softly is what they were asked to do. Furthermore, by starting at one-quarter volume, students have a chance to see that they will not be the only ones participating; this builds their confidence. Next, I bring them up to half volume, three-quarters volume, and finally full volume.

After the students have successfully performed the participation task and are feeling confident, give them an opportunity to try it without your leadership. Tell the kids that you are going to assist them with the activity one more time so they can practice and that they will then be on their own the next time through. This increases their focus and adds a little variety to the activity.

In cases where only a portion of the group is participating, do not ask for more participation from the group as a whole. If you do, generally those already participating will increase the intensity of their participation and those not participating will continue their lackluster performance. Instead, compliment the group that is participating and encourage the group that is not.

If the entire audience is participating, but a little timidly, and you want to pump the enthusiasm level up a little, avoid using words like *louder*. If you ask a group to sing louder, some students will invariably begin to yell. This spreads like wildfire. Instead, use phrases like *a fuller sound* or *participation from everyone*.

Never attempt to browbeat the audience into participation. If they are not participating, it's probably because they are afraid they might be judged *uncool* by their peers. (This phenomenon is usually restricted to the older students. Given an example to follow, K-3 students will almost always participate.) In dealing with the *coolness factor*, you must show understanding rather than scorn or ridicule. For example, if I see the coolness factor at play while conducting the vocal warm-up exercise described earlier, I take a moment to discuss it with the students. I say:

> As I look around the room, I see a lot of students that would like to be singing but are afraid to. I know what this fear is all about—it's a very real thing. Sometimes we're afraid that if we join in, we'll be the only one doing so, and that can be embarrassing. Sometimes we're afraid that someone might look at us and think we're uncool for participating. There are a couple of things you can do to help each other get over these fears and begin participating. First, you can make sure you are looking straight ahead—not turning around looking at the students behind you. I know the reason some of you are looking behind you is to see if others are singing, giving you the courage to join in. The problem is that if someone is a little afraid, but is trying to get beyond their fear, it makes it harder when people are looking at them. Secondly, we can trust each other to keep a commitment to sing, even if it's just a little. This way, you'll know you won't be the only one. Let's try it again at one-quarter volume with everyone keeping the commitment.

After singing the refrain again at one-quarter volume, I compliment those who kept the commitment and sang even though they perhaps were still a little afraid. I tell them that their courage is going to make it easier for others to join in. As the audience's participation level increases, I tell them that they have done so well in turning things around that now those who are not participating may have to worry about being the only person who is *not* singing.

I believe this approach works because it identifies the problem, validates the children's concerns, and proposes a solution that empowers the students to solve the problem themselves.

## Selecting volunteers for individual participation

Selecting a capable volunteer from the audience for an individual participation activity can be a tricky matter. After you explain what the volunteer will be doing and ask those who would like to give it a try to raise their hands, look for a poised, together-looking student who has his hand confidently raised. Avoid students who are wildly waving their hands in the air; this is often more indicative of a desperate desire to be up on stage than a confidence that they can perform the task. Also, avoid those who have their hands half way up in the air, their attention divided between you and the student beside them into whose ear they are whispering. Another approach is to ask a teacher to select the volunteer by saying something like, "I'd like to ask Mr. Miller (you can get a specific teacher's name in advance of the program) to select for me a student who has good poise and confidence to come forward for this activity." The teachers are in a much better position than you to select an appropriate student, especially if you're relatively inexperienced in selecting volunteers.

## Giving instructions

When providing instructions for students in the course of the program, make them clear, concise, and complete. The result of poorly delivered instructions is wasted time and broken momentum. The surest way to clarity and brevity is to prepare a script for the instructions in advance. Each step of the instructions should provide information regarding not only what to do, but how and when to do it. Edit the instructions, honing them down to the fewest possible words. Rehearse and memorize the script as you would a performance piece. During the program, provide instructions in their entirety before beginning the activity; giving additional instructions after the activity is in progress is very difficult. For example, when we give students a chance to stand up and stretch about half way through the program, we provide instructions regarding re-seating *before* they are permitted to stand up. If we didn't provide the instructions in advance, we'd literally have to shout over the commotion to get them down again.

In giving instructions, the difference between what works and what does not is often subtle. Observe how students respond to your instructions. Analyze what specific words or phrases get the desired results. Conversely, watch for words or phrases that draw blank looks from the kids or create confusion.

## Getting appropriate applause

*We try to teach the kids not to cheer and shout.* - Tim O'Brien, Principal, Issaquah Valley ES, Issaquah WA

It might seem strange, but often students are not certain when and where they should applaud in a program. Furthermore, they often don't know if it's appropriate to whistle and cheer in addition to clapping. Knowing when and how to show appreciation in a particular type of performance is part of what students should be learning by experiencing your program. Don't be hesitant to discuss appropriate applause at the beginning of the program. It may seem a little egotistical discussing your own applause, but when an audience doesn't know when and how to show their appreciation, it is awkward for the audience and performers alike.

## Clapping along

In programs incorporating music, students will often spontaneously begin clapping along to the beat. Although in some situations this is appropriate and even welcome, in other situations it is very distracting. Once started, it will not stop of its own accord. The problem can be dealt with in a preventative manner early in the program: tell the audience that sometimes it will be okay to clap along, but that other times they will need to be able to hear and it's hard to hear above clapping. Then inform them of a cue that you have devised to let them know when it is appropriate to clap along and when it's not. (The cue may be something as simple as a member of the ensemble initiating the clapping themselves and then lowering their hands slowly, palms down, when the clapping should cease.) For programs where it is seldom, if ever, appropriate to clap along, it may be better not to bring the subject up; if clapping along does occur, simply pause at the next opportunity and explain to the children why it detracts from the program and ask them not to do it.

In any case where a genuine expression of enthusiasm is getting in the way, be careful not to reflect any irritation or displeasure, thus embarrassing students or causing them to be inhibited in responding to the show. Channel and guide their enthusiasm, don't squash it.

## Asking questions

*Be careful about getting into situations where you are asking individual questions of the kids unless you really know how to manage it. You've got five hundred kids raising their hands; now you've got to pick through them...a lot of time can be expended with minimal return.* - Cory Crawford, Principal, Fruitland ES, Puyallup WA

Done properly, occasionally asking some questions of the audience is an effective way to review the educational aspects of your program or refocus attention. Always tell the audience beforehand that you'll be asking some questions, that you want them to raise their hands *after they have heard the question*, and that you'll be calling on students who are sitting quietly with their hands up. Do not acknowledge students who call out answers, wildly wave their hands, or exhibit other inappropriate behavior; doing so will only cause the behavior to spread and lead to a loss of control. Ask questions that have a single correct answer. For example, "How many strings does a violin have?" rather than, "What does a violin sound like?"

Asking questions of the audience as a whole and having them respond in unison can also be effective. Tell the audience that you will be asking questions that have one-word answers, that

110

you will allow a moment for them to formulate an answer, and that upon a specified signal (a cupped ear, a phrase such as "And the answer is...," or similar cue) they should respond together. Yes-or-no, true-and-false, or multiple-choice questions lend themselves very well to group Q&A.

## Regaining attention

If the audience becomes restless in spite of all you have done to keep them engaged and focused, ask for their cooperation—let them know that the program can't go on until order is restored. Here are some lines I have found effective:

"I'm going to wait for just a moment until I have all eyes and ears up front."

"We're going to wait for just a moment because I see some students who are having trouble hearing because the people next to them are talking. Remember there shouldn't be any talking during the program."

"At the beginning of the program I mentioned what good listeners you were. Well, that's going to be especially important on this next song because the words tell a story."

If lines like these don't work, a quick game of *Simon Says* is often effective. The room will quiet down quickly because the students need to be able to hear in order to play the game. Wrap the game up by saying, "Simon says put your hands in your lap, look at the performers, and breathe through your nose." (It's impossible to breathe through your nose and talk at the same time.) Once you have succeeded in regaining the students' attention, be prepared to move on with the program without further delay.

Many artists use a cue or signal—a sign, word, or phrase—to indicate to the audience that everyone's attention needs to be focused up front. Such a system will prevent you from falling into a cycle of nagging, constantly asking for the audience's

111

attention. Before the program, ask the principal if there is already a school-wide cue program intact; if so, use the school's particular sign or signal. The use of the signal or cue should be explained to the audience early in the program, when audience expectations are being set. To maintain the effectiveness of the cue system, praise and thank the audience whenever they respond to the cue.

If you have a chronically distracted audience, you must judge the point at which you should give up trying to restore order, go on with the program, and make the best of it. Once in a while something happens—snow begins to fall outside, the recess bell rings, or a fire alarm goes off in the middle of the program (yes, this has happened to us)—that irreversibly distracts the audience.

**Positive reinforcement**

Whenever the audience successfully follows directions or meets expectations, compliment them. For example, if they listen to a piece especially well after participating on the previous one, I say, "Not only are you excellent singers but you are also outstanding listeners." Then after a few more songs I say, "Before we go on I want you to know what a terrific audience you have been so far—everybody is participating well, listening well and doing an excellent job of following directions." By doing this, not only have I complimented them on specific accomplishments, but I have indirectly reminded them of the audience expectations as well.

It is important to understand the distinction between positive reinforcement and false praise, particularly since no one knows the difference between the two better than children. Positive reinforcement does not mean telling the audience that they did something well when they in fact did not. Nor does positive reinforcement preclude offering suggestions regarding improvement. It is possible to be truthful, suggest improvements, and be positive at the same time. For example, if you are getting a less than satisfactory level of participation you can say something like, "I see lots people singing out there, and you sound just great. I can't wait to see what it sounds like with *everybody* participating. Let's try it again!" In saying this, you will compliment those who are doing well and encourage those who are not. And you have done so without overlooking the fact that a portion of the audience is not participating, or falsely praising the group as a whole. If you fall into the trap of false praise, the audience will tune you out in a matter of minutes.

Follow these guidelines in using positive reinforcement:

- Make the praise specific. "Great job of remembering all the words to that song" is much more effective than "nice job."

- Compliment students' abilities or talents in addition to their efforts. For example, "You sound great. You are such talented singers."

- Make sure your spirit, facial expression, and enthusiasm match your words of praise. Praise delivered in a hum-drum or perfunctory fashion is quickly tuned out by children.

- Avoid comparing students or classes to one another: "The second-graders are doing almost as well as the third-graders."

- Avoid tempering your praise with the word *but*: "I see lots of people participating but it would sure sound better if everyone would join in." This type of phrasing puts the emphasis on what's wrong, reduces the impact of the effort put forth by those who are participating, and is ultimately a negative statement.

### When you goof in a big way

Sooner or later, one day you will slip and say something potentially very disruptive. For example, on one unfortunate occasion I got my consonants mixed up and instead of saying,

113

"On this first part...," I said, "On this pirst fart...." I said it loud and clear—it was definitely out there. I immediately realized what I had done, but looked straight ahead and continued without missing a beat. There was no disturbance. Afterwards many students probably discussed among themselves the fact that they were quite certain they had heard me say *fart*. One can only imagine what would have happened if I had faltered (no, not farted), turned red, and the audience had started giggling. My only option would have been to have laughed right along with them and then set out to regain control.

## REMEDIAL TECHNIQUES

On occasion, even in a top-quality program presented by highly skilled artists, there will be students whose behavior is inappropriate. Knowing how to effectively deal with disruptive students will significantly limit their impact on the program.

### Non-verbal intervention

In many cases, a meaningful look, a head shaking "no," and a follow-up smile will take care of an individual student's misbehavior. There is an important prerequisite to this non-verbal approach: the artist must constantly scan the crowd, locate trouble spots, and then catch the eye of the offender. (Catching the eye of an errant student is relatively easy: just like the motorist scanning an intersection for law enforcement before racing to beat a yellow light, kids will almost always make eye contact with the authority figure to see if they are being watched before proceeding with an inappropriate activity. Furthermore, after proceeding with the activity, they will continue to make eye contact intermittently to ascertain that their misbehavior has not been detected.) Once you have caught the student's eye, give him a look that says "I see what you are doing," followed by a head shake that says "knock it off!" Then keep your eyes on the student for a moment or two to let them know that you will be continuing to monitor their

114

behavior. After moving your eyes away for a few moments—and scanning for the next trouble spot—establish eye contact with the student once again. If he is behaving himself, give him a smile that says "thank you."

In addition to providing an opportunity to deal with inappropriate activities before they spread, constantly scanning the crowd, will prevent many such activities from getting started in the first place.

## Verbal intervention

*You've got to have high expectations. You can't allow little groups of kids to be jabbering. I don't think there is anything wrong with stopping and letting the kids know that you have to have everybody's attention—that the program is not going to work if you've got ten kids back there passing baseball cards back and forth.* -
Jim Eisenhardt, Principal, Yelm Prairie ES, Yelm WA

*One of the reasons we have assemblies is to teach kids how to behave at performances...Artists can help our cause by reinforcing our efforts.* - Newt Adams, Principal, Clarkmoor ES, Tacoma WA

On occasion, non-verbal intervention will be ineffective. The next step is verbal intervention: directly addressing the audience and requesting an end to the activity. Before employing verbal intervention to terminate an inappropriate activity, calculate your chances of success by asking yourself the following questions:

- Is the activity limited to a small group of students, or is it widespread?

- Is the activity something that is readily detectable by the teachers? Can they identify students who continue with the activity after you ask for its termination?

- Is the activity something that is so tempting to other students that calling attention to it will only make matters worse?

The fewer the number of students involved in the inappropriate activity, the better your chances of successfully terminating it. Obviously, dealing with problems early on helps you control this factor. Waiting until you have a large portion of the audience involved in a number of inappropriate activities makes the restoration of order very difficult, if not impossible.

If the inappropriate activity is readily detectable, your chances of terminating the misbehavior are good. After you make a request for the termination of the activity, teachers will monitor their students and, if the misbehavior continues, nab the students responsible. On the other hand, if it is difficult for teachers to identify students who persist with the activity, your chances of success are significantly reduced—experienced trouble makers can make sudden loud noises, stomp their feet on bleachers, whistle, and conduct other distracting activities with very little risk of detection.

If the activity is something very tempting to other students, the power of suggestion will work against you the moment you mention the activity. Whistling, scrunching chairs on the floor, stomping feet on bleachers are a few examples. With these activities, employ verbal intervention only as a last resort. Generally, teachers are well aware of the contagious nature of these activities and will take swift action, terminating the misbehavior before it spreads.

Four or five inappropriate activities comprise ninety-five percent of the misbehavior encountered in assembly programs. Described below are common inappropriate activities, along with suggestions for dealing with them if non-verbal intervention proves ineffective.

**Mocking**

Sometimes students, having decided that the program is beneath them, begin making fun of the artists. This behavior is usually restricted to sixth-graders. Mocking takes many forms, but by far the most common is swaying back and forth to music. It is difficult for the artists to ignore—nobody likes to be made fun of. One day, in a wonderfully spontaneous moment, my partner came up with a very effective response. It was honest, sincere, and dealt with the problem head on. She said, "There is a group of students in the back, swaying back and forth to the music, and I find it very distracting. I'd like to ask you not to do that." It worked. They stopped immediately, and there was no more swaying for the duration of the program. Best of all, it didn't alienate the students or put them on the spot. It wasn't necessary for my partner to point out that the reason the behavior distracted her was because it was rude and mean-spirited. They could have argued with that: "We're not being rude, we were just getting into the music." But they couldn't argue that the swaying didn't distract her. We have used this approach ever since with unfailing success.

Other forms of mockery employed by students include mimicking the words of a singer, the movements of a dancer, or the gestures of a speaker in an unflattering manner. This type of mockery is less of a problem than swaying: it is not as readily seen by other students, and does not have the same contagious quality. If ignored, the problem often goes away. If it doesn't, and non-verbal intervention fails, I have had good results looking directly at the students involved and saying, "One of the things I hate to do most in a program is embarrass someone who is misbehaving. I see some students acting in a very disruptive way. I'm not going to point them out—they know who they are. But I *am* going to warn them that if they continue, I will have no choice but to stop the program and ask them to go sit beside their teacher." It is important to say this as though you truly were concerned about having to embarrass the students involved; do *not* say it in a threatening way. Also, never indicate that you are going to ask a teacher to take action; they may resent such a request. (Notice that I indicate I will ask the students to go sit by their teacher rather than saying that I will ask the teacher to pull the students or take other action.) Only one time have I had to follow through and direct a student to go sit by her teacher. It was an awkward moment, but the audience (and the performers) were able to enjoy the remainder of the program, unhampered by the student's disruptive behavior.

I have also taken the opportunity during a break to go out and talk to a student or group of students about disruptive behavior, telling them I don't want to embarrass them or get them in trouble by talking with their teacher, but they must agree to cease with the misbehavior. Often we seal the deal by shaking on it.

## Yelling

Sometimes when students are participating verbally—singing, responding in unison to questions, repeating phrases—a few students will begin yelling. If this happens I say, "I see some students who are straining their voices. Remember, we never want to sing so loudly that it sounds like yelling." Other times I work in a discussion of musical dynamics and explain that I would like them to sing in a medium-soft voice on the song.

## Whistling

Whistling is a tough problem to deal with. Sometimes a very young student will innocently whistle along to music in a program, not knowing how distracting it is to the artist and those around him. Other times students will whistle in a deliberate attempt to annoy other students or the performers or to draw attention to themselves. In either case—because there is no lip movement involved in whistling—it can be very difficult to identify the source of the problem. First, ignore it and see if it goes away—don't call attention to it; kids love to whistle, and the mere mention of the word will often result in half the group whistling and the other half trying. If the problem doesn't go away or begins to spread, you'll have no choice but to stop and explain that the whistling is distractive and must stop. If it continues after you resume the program, teachers will often get up, scan the crowd, and assist in remedying the situation.

## Social (or anti-social) activities

Small groups of students sometimes become involved in playing with or passing among themselves, toys, coins, clothes, and other personal items. If the situation is left unremedied, the circle of students involved rapidly grows in size. If non-verbal intervention does not work, take the same measures as suggested for mocking. The same applies to students involved in hitting one another or invading one another's personal space.

## Teacher support

You will almost invariably have the support of the teachers in dealing with disruptive behavior. Once you mention a problem, they will often stand up and monitor their class to make sure one of their kids is not the culprit. Since having the teachers on your side is so valuable, be sure not to do or say anything during the program that undermines that support. It's easy to do this in a subtle way without even realizing it. For example, in a program I was observing, the artist, trying to gets the audience to respond to her more enthusiastically, told the kids, "Don't worry about those teachers sitting right there beside you—this is not a classroom. It's okay for you to call out responses and answers without raising your hands first." Though she didn't intend it, there was a subtle sense of overriding the teachers' authority, creating an us-against-them feeling. Later in the program, as the kids got more and more out of control, the teachers seemed to have adopted an it's-your-problem attitude as the artist struggled to restore order.

Taking a no-nonsense approach to misbehavior makes the teachers' job during the assembly much easier. We have received many favorable comments from teachers regarding the fact that we set expectations and enforce them.

## Be assertive

Don't allow your program to be diminished or ruined by a

handful of disruptive students because you're afraid or intimidated. Failure to deal with inappropriate behavior will quickly take the fun out of performing in schools and destroy your reputation. With all audience misbehavior, there are only two reasons not to take remedial action: one, because there is little or no chance of success, or two, because there is a likelihood that remedial action will only make things worse. Fear or intimidation are not good reasons for inaction.

## How NOT to do it

Sometimes, in learning how to do something, it's helpful to have an example of how not to do it. The following is an excerpt from a review of an assembly program:

About two-thirds of the way through, an actor dressed as an age-old storyteller appears on stage and indicates, tongue in cheek, that he is going to tell a love story. The audience groans, reciprocating the tongue-in-cheek spirit. The storyteller, ignoring their sentiments, says he doesn't care if they don't want to hear the story; he will tell it anyway. As he begins the story, the kids drown him out, crying, "No, No, No." He stops, waits a moment, and then tries again. Once more, the kids drown him out, and once more, he stops, waits, and begins again. Thinking he is still kidding, I begin to wonder how he is going to break this cycle. Suddenly it is apparent that he is no longer joking: remaining in character, he tells the kids that if they don't be quiet, he will point them out individually and ask their teacher to remove them from the show. "Just to show you that I am serious," he says, "I am going to get one of the *real people* to tell you so." Walking over to a teacher at the end of the front row, he grabs her by the hand, pulls her out of her chair, and says, "You tell them that I am serious." The teacher, embarrassed and on the spot, finally says in a voice so soft it can't be heard past the second row, "He wants your undivided attention." Returning to the stage, the storyteller tries once more to begin the story. Several first-graders still don't get it and begin groaning and imploring him not to tell a love story. This time the storyteller tries to out-shout them. He has no microphone and the attempt fails. Turning on his heel, he goes behind the curtain and, after a long delay—an accompanist all the while continuing with background music—comes back out without his mask and chews the kids out for being rude. He tells the kids that although there are times when he wants this sort of back-and-forth response from the audience, this is definitely not one of those times. In a rather demeaning manner, he adds, "When I told you I was going to tell a love story, it was a joke—which you didn't get." He goes behind the curtain again, dons his mask, returns, and begins the story once more. The audience—now crushed and subdued—is dead quiet. Even during parts of the story intended to be humorous, the children are afraid to respond. A short way into the story, two actors appear, playing roles in the story. When their roles call for them to argue with one another, the storyteller comments that they are "being just as rude as this audience." A few moments later, at the end of the skit, he unintentionally drops the book from which he is reading and mutters, "This is the day when everything went wrong."

Well, everything did indeed go wrong. Let's take a look at the reasons. To begin with, there should have been a signal to let the kids know when it was time to stop responding vocally—which they had been encouraged to do throughout the program. For example, a big *shush* face could have appeared over the curtain as a signal that it was time to be quiet. Second, unless absolutely unavoidable, the actor portraying the storyteller should not have been the person trying to regain control. Furthermore, he should not have remained in character. When an artist remains in character while taking remedial action, it is very difficult for the audience to know whether or not the remedial action is part of the skit. Third, when the storyteller finally stopped the program, the accompanist should have stopped as well; the continuation of the music contributed to the audience's confusion over what was part of the skit and what was not. Fourth, the storyteller's threat to have disruptive students removed from the show was one he could not have followed through with—there were too many students involved. Where would the teachers have taken the students? Who would have supervised them for the remainder of the show? Fifth, putting a teacher on the spot by asking her to address the audience was a mistake. With the crowd out of control and no access to a microphone, her response could not help but be the ineffective one that it was. Sixth, trying to out-shout the audience was an error: he had no microphone and he was outnumbered five-hundred to one—he set himself up for defeat. Seventh, after coming down hard on the audience, the storyteller should have worked immediately toward restoring a good rapport with the audience; the comment about the audience's rudeness, in the course of the next skit, only further diminished what little rapport remained.

◆ ◆ ◆

**Ending the program**

Somewhere in the last minutes of your program, let the audience know that the program is about to end. If appropriate, thank the students for being a good audience, and thank the teachers and staff for their help in preparing the students for the program. Remind the students to remain seated after the end of the program. Tell them to wait and see if the principal comes forward to dismiss them and, if not, to look to their teachers for a signal before standing up and returning to their classrooms.

**Summary**

In order to present a program effectively, an artist must do the following:

● set an educational tone for the program

● articulate audience expectations

- speak in a manner appropriate for the oldest students
- keep a fast pace
- inspire group participation
- select capable volunteers for individual participation segments
- provide clear, concise, and complete instructions
- effectively conduct a question-and-answer session
- regain audience attention if the audience becomes distracted
- effectively use positive reinforcement
- be assertive in taking remedial action (both verbal and nonverbal) if necessary.

See the interviews in Chapter 11 and Chapter 12 for additional discussion of program presentation techniques.

The primary purpose of this chapter is to make clear the necessity of setting an educational tone, taking charge of the assembly from the moment you're introduced, and effectively dealing with any disruptions that might occur during the course of the program. In the process of doing these things, don't forget to have fun! A kind, loving, joyful approach is absolutely mandatory; hard-hearted authoritarianism will not be effective. Strive to combine the techniques and skills discussed in this chapter with the approach toward children outlined in Chapter 3; it's a powerful combination.

# CHAPTER 10
# The Sale of Recordings and Publications

Following your presentation, you can significantly enhance your profit line through the sale of recordings or publications. However, you must proceed with caution. If the presentation was sponsored by an arts commission, there may be a clause in the commission's contract that prohibits such sales. In addition, many school districts have policies restricting the selling of merchandise by outside vendors during school hours. Adhering to the following guidelines will prevent principals from raising objections to the sale of publications and recordings:

- Sell to teachers only, never to students.

- Sell only materials appropriate for educational purposes. Do not sell T-shirts, hats, coffee cups, etc.

- Make the announcement regarding the availability of merchandise brief and low key.

- Make it extremely quick and easy for teachers to obtain the merchandise. Having a credit system, which eliminates the need for writing checks or handling money, is the key.

---

## CASSETTE INVOICE

Thank you for your purchase of cassette albums as indicated:

__ *Two Sides of Dave & Cindy* ($9.00)

__ *Blossom* ($9.00)

__ Both the above titles ($15.00)

Please make check payable to *Dave & Cindy* and send payment to:

**Dave & Cindy**
**P.O. Box 1407**
**Orient WA  99141**

To insure proper credit please provide the following information:

Name: _____

School: _____

City:  _____

If you have already paid, please accept our apologies. Please write "paid" across this invoice and mail it back to us.

Thank You!

---

Figure 10-1: An invoice given to teachers at the time of sale, allowing them to make payment by mail.

Here is a system my duo has used successfully for years:

1. Near the end of the program we make a brief announcement indicating that tapes are available to teachers at the cost of nine dollars. We tell teachers they may get a tape today by simply coming forward and requesting one and that they may take care of payment later by mail.

2. When teachers come forward and ask for a tape, we write down their name and hand them a tape wrapped with an invoice (see figure 10-1) and return envelope. This delays the teachers' return to the classroom by only a few seconds.

3. If students make inquiries, we tell them it is against school policy for us to sell them a tape. If a teacher asks how her students can obtain tapes, we provide her with order forms.

Most teachers make payment within a few days. Those that fail to pay within 30 days receive a billing. (Getting their name and the amount they owe at the time of sale is all the billing information you need: you can send the invoice to their attention at the school's address.) We have an extremely low default rate—perhaps two percent. We believe the credit system is largely responsible for the thousands of cassettes we sell to teachers annually.

126

# CHAPTER 11
# Young Audiences, Inc.

*Young Audiences* is a nationwide organization dedicated to bringing the performing arts into America's schools. Artists on the organization's rosters present over 55,000 programs to more than 6 million children each year. In 1994 President Clinton awarded Young Audiences the National Medal of Arts for the organization's contributions to arts education.

Young Audiences strives to integrate artistry of the highest caliber, the discoveries of child psychology, and the latest in education research and technique in their approach to arts-in-education programming. In pursuing this goal, local chapters offer ongoing training for participating artists. In addition, the organization's *Arts-in-Education Institute* periodically brings together artists, educators, and YA personnel from around the country to collaborate on improving program design and presentation skills.

In addition to providing valuable training, the organization also handles the artists' marketing and booking, doing all the contact and scheduling work with the schools. With local chapters in virtually every area of the country, YA offers considerable opportunity for artists who wish to make performing in schools a serious part of their career. (See the Appendix for contact information.)

Larry Stein, Director of Program Development for National Young Audiences, granted the following interview. Larry is both an accomplished artist and experienced educator. He has presented programs at Carnegie Hall, taught at the elementary, secondary, and college levels and has served as a consultant to numerous arts organizations. Larry is a founding member of the *Repercussion Unit* and producer for Robey Records and PAL Productions. His music can also be heard on the German label, CMP Records. With Young Audiences since 1978, Larry directs the organization's *Arts-in-Education Institute,* a professional-development program for artists and teachers, currently operating in nine sites across the nation.

Larry sometimes offers different perspectives than those you have read in previous chapters of this book, providing a welcome and valuable second opinion on matters such as audience management, the development of NPC segments, and program presentation.

*A* indicates the author, *S* indicates Stein.

## The unique aspects of a YA performance

A: What are some of the qualities that make a YA performance distinctly different from other assembly programs being presented in schools?

S: First and foremost, YA attempts to select artists that represent the best artistry available in the community for their particular art form. That is the primary issue. Before an artist is put on the roster, or before they go through extensive training with YA program staff on how to relate with kids, they need to demonstrate a high skill level in their art form and a commitment to their art form as a pure entity.

Second, would be the level of professionalism of the artist, both in terms of how they deal with the YA chapter and how they deal with basic issues of punctuality, demeanor, and other areas of professional conduct. In many cases, the artist is the only representative of YA on a particular day or series of days in which they are doing programs. The artist needs to be someone that the chapter can feel comfortable with in terms of representing not only the chapter but all the other artists in the entire organization.

A third thing that distinguishes a YA presentation is that it is presented by artists who love kids and are willing to put the child, as opposed to their own individual egos, at the focus of the program. Now, that is somewhat of a paradox to the first thing I addressed, the artist's skill level, because if you are going to be an artist of the highest quality, you've spent a lot of time developing your own ego and your own art form in order to be out there performing, and it's all about you, the artist. We're looking to balance that sense of confidence and enthusiasm with a real respect for the kids and a commitment to their empowerment. That's the hard part: how to match those two things—how to get someone who can hold on to their own artistic integrity, but at the same time not set the audience off by giving them the sense that this is something so special to the artist that the audience is excluded from getting inside of it or accessing it either as spectators or potential artists themselves. I think it is this balance that identifies the best in YA artists and is what all YA programs strive for.

Also very important for YA artists of the future—as we consider the trends that are pushing the educational reform movement as it pertains to arts-in-education in the schools—is their willingness to allow other people into the design process. Will they allow the YA chapter consultant or even school personnel to affect new program ideas? And how willing is the artist to embrace content changes to address issues about which the schools are concerned?

## Audience management

A: I know that YA helps artists incorporate basic teaching techniques into their programs. Can you explain some of these techniques as they relate to several areas, the first of which is getting the kind of audience behavior the artist desires?

S: I generally find that the issue of audience control is not one that should be addressed directly. If the myriad of other presentation techniques are used correctly, inevitably audience control won't be a problem. For instance, (1) if there is adequate opportunity for the kids to interact with the artist in a variety of ways throughout the program; (2) if the artist employs what we call a *handle question* where whatever questions the artists asks of the audience are not asked as a way of assessing whether the kids knew the answer before the artist got there or not (which many artists tend to do with questions like, "Who can tell me the name of this instrument?") but a question that would stimulate the child to look for the answer in the next performance piece or the next activity, and as that piece or activity is finished the artist restates that *handle question* (that's why it's called a handle question: because it holds the piece up on both sides) empowering the child to look within the activity or performance piece, using hints or clues the artist may give them, to formulate an answer; (3) if there is an interchange that is ongoing in what we call the *dialogue method*, that is, if there is a real dialogue going on between the artist and the audience—even if it's a large audience; (4) if the audience's responses are valued, meaning that whatever answer a student or a group of students may give an artist—the artist must, of course, ask the question in the right way—that answer is made a part of the forward movement of the program; (5) if the pacing is correct and the pieces are related to each other, with the transitions from one to the other making sense; (6) if there is a sense of positive attitude, love, and enthusiasm being exuded by all the artists on the stage; if all these kinds of things come together with an excellence in artistry, there will not be a need to create any kind of classroom management or discipline technique. If these elements are not present or dealt with in the correct way, then some standard techniques drawn from classroom management principles can be employed: signals, rewards, techniques such as going up to the microphone and acting like it's switched off, which tends to quiet the room down to a whisper, using the element of surprise, creating pseudo conflict on stage, such as acting out an argument between members of the ensemble, and other techniques. Whenever these techniques are necessary to control the audience, then that means that the program has some faults in other areas. So I tend not to focus on these management techniques in and of themselves because it takes the focus off the real issue, which is program design.

## Engaging the audience

A: What are some standard teaching techniques that can be used to engage the audience in watching and/or listening to non-performance content in the program?

S: Avoiding predictability would be one technique. For example, when a program is presented by an ensemble, it often includes the introduction of each of the instruments. There are a variety of ways of introducing the instruments, some of which are very predictable. If you're going to go around from the clarinet to the flute to the oboe, by the time you get to the third or fourth instrument, regardless of how engaging the person doing the talking might be, predictability becomes a problem. Here's a way around this: in a woodwind quintet—where the French horn player is kind of the odd man out, or odd woman out, because the horn is the only instrument made of brass—have the horn player constantly interrupt the others as they are talking about their instruments, in order to talk about the horn. This sets up a conflict in a theatrical kind of way that gets kids in the audience pulling for the horn player. Setting up those kinds of things, throughout a period of time, keeps the interest on what's finally going to happen. It gets the kids wondering: "When are we going to get to hear the French horn part. What piece of music is going to come up that will validate the fact that the horn player was interrupting the other musicians?"

A: What about keeping interest during the pieces themselves?

131

S: Any particular hints or clues to certain things that may be coming up in the piece will keep the kids motivated to find it—they want to succeed. Relating back to the example with the French horn, they also want the horn player, the person considered the odd man out, to succeed. So the setup keeps them motivated to follow it through.

**Audience participation**

A: What about techniques to get the audience, particularly fifth- and sixth-graders, beyond the *inhibition factor* to enthusiastic participation?

S: You have to model the participation first. If the artist is particularly enthusiastic and the other members of the ensemble join in, that will kind of get the audience to deal with it also. The other thing is for the participation to be meaningful participation as opposed to token participation and for the participation to make a difference to the forward movement of the program. The kids can see through it when the primary reason for participating is because it makes the artist look good in the eyes of the teachers and principal and doesn't necessarily move the program along. If you are trying to get the audience to sing along, and they know that it doesn't really make any difference to the forward movement of the program whether you have 100 voices singing along or 200, they won't be motivated to participate, especially the older ones. They have to feel that their participation makes a difference to the outcome of the program. As an example, several years ago I was presenting a program about making instruments out of second-hand materials—pots and pans and that kind of stuff. We had a couple of tables laid out with these things. In the middle of the program there comes a time for the kids to identify which types of instruments they would like us to play—metals or woods or whatever. In this way, the kids would direct us in which direction the show would take, and they were aware of this dynamic. Due to the makeup of this particular audience, it was really tough to get the kids to want to raise their hands at all. After a few minutes of no participation, I looked to my partner and said, "Well, if no one is going to choose which instrument we're going to play next, let's get packed and head back to LA, because the show's over." Within a few seconds of starting to pack up, hands were shooting up all over the place. That's a dramatic response to the situation, but it showed me that you have to give the kids the sense that they are affecting the outcome of the program; it's the primary difference between a live show and a tape or CD.

A: When selecting individual members of the audience to come forward to participate in a performance or demonstration, what are some things artists can do to help insure they select a student who can do whatever it is they need them to do?

S: The first thing they can do is to make sure they demonstrate whatever it is they want the student(s) to do before making the selection. If you ask for volunteers without doing this, the kids who have their hands up will be those who just want to volunteer, regardless of what they might be asked to do. Furthermore, when you finally do show the volunteers what you want them to do, the rest of the audience loses focus. They will only care about what volunteers will be doing when they think they might get picked: they want to pay attention so that if they get picked, they'll know what to do. The second thing is harder to do. You look into the eyes of the kids whose hands are up and try to determine if they are connecting in a way that is really about what you just demonstrated or if they're shaking their hand wildly just because they just want to be up there. Just having their hand up is not the clue. You must get a sense of whether they are with you or not.

**Writing narratives (or not)**

A: Let's assume an artist has completed the process of gathering together the repertoire for a show and is now sitting down to create narratives to tie the pieces all together. What advice can you offer him in regards to the creation of these narratives?

S: I think the artist in this case is still a couple of steps away from the writing process. In fact, we have to get away from the idea that an educational program is nothing more than a series of pieces with some well-articulated narrative between them. That's one way of teaching about an art, but there are other ways of doing it without using narrative, like the example earlier regarding the French horn player. While using narrative is perhaps the easiest route—and certainly the first route most artists take—it can become predictable and sets the artist up as an authority figure telling the kids something they should know; it doesn't necessarily move toward their empowerment. Methods such as dialogue between the artist and the audience, activities, and theatrical techniques can help you avoid these traps. I suggest that you not begin by writing narrative. One approach might be to take a look at each of the pieces you have gathered together for the show and ask yourself, "What is it that I like about this piece? Why did I choose it? Why do I think it works? What are the salient characteristics of this piece? What does it do? What does it show? Is it funny? Does it show off the role of a particular member of the ensemble? Does the content embody some sort of a message?" Now, you'll end up with quite a list for each piece or work—much more than can be dealt with in the show. At some point in the editing process that follows, you need to define the main theme of the program. Once you have a basic idea of what your program theme is going to be—which may emerge as a result of this inventory of what you have in each piece or was something you knew going in—that becomes the editing tool to determine which characteristics of which pieces you are going to focus on. Most of the characteristics of each piece will have nothing to do with the the educational objective, pacing considerations, or thematic content of the program—they'll be outside of it. So, at that point you pare away: you try to identify maybe one or two salient characteristics for each piece that will support the educational theme of the program. The next question is, are there ways to get the point across without talking about it? That's one difference between an artist and a teacher: conveying ideas through the art form without talking about it. It turns out that, in many of these programs, there is plenty of talking anyway. I mean, this is really almost a futile attempt, but it's something that I push because even if it's only one or two concepts out of ten that you can present this way, it makes the program go from good to great.

The next thing you look at, after you have listed the salient characteristics of each piece, is determining an order for the pieces. Would the order of the pieces be different if you focused more on the salient characteristics of each piece rather purely on the repertoire itself? It doesn't necessarily mean that you will go with either one, but it's good to see if they line up. This is all very important before writing, because it will effect the transitions in terms of what you say and how you get from one piece to the other.

Once you are clear on the educational objective of the program, you understand what specific concepts you are going to be dealing with in each of the pieces, and you have worked out ways of presenting some of these concepts through performances rather than talking, then you can start doing the program in front of kids, letting a natural improvisation take place in doing the transitions. You can record these performances, review them, and then begin cleaning them up. Now, this doesn't work for everybody; some people need to have more of it scripted before doing these initial performances. The danger of using a set script that is too cleaned up and polished is that, during performance, it doesn't look like the kids affect the outcome of the program—it doesn't look to them like the show they're seeing today is any different than the show that the artist did yesterday or will do tomorrow at another school. So the somewhat spontaneous approach that I am suggesting—if you are very clear about what your program is about and you have an order that serves the development of the educational objective—gives the audience a sense that it is a much more relaxed, informal kind of performance. But a lot of people can't do that. For those people who are not comfortable with this approach, we suggest they write out a kickoff line for each segment and then improvise from there. It gives the performance much more of a fresh, spontaneous approach than having it all memorized. It's this approach that kids in a live situation react to in a positive way. It's very different from something that feels carefully scripted. Other artists may be able to start out with narratives that are totally scripted, become completely comfortable with them, and then begin a loosening-up process that will make the delivery more conversational. None of these things are locked in stone one way or the other. It's a balance of many of these techniques and the different personalities of the artists developing the programs.

**Curriculum connections**

A: Many artists are attempting to make connections in their program to non-art curriculum. What things can they do to develop connections that are meaningful and valid from an educator's perspective?

S: We are working on a curriculum-integration initiative that will engage teachers in the design process so that artists do not presuppose that they can design connections that will be on the mark. In some of the programs I present, we've begun experimenting with a process of providing teachers in the audience with an outline giving concise information about each of the pieces in the program. We ask them to take notes regarding any connections to classroom curriculum that occur to them during the course of the show. Afterwards, we can incorporate these connections in the program or, more likely, into the prep/follow up materials. Again, you can see the need for the artist to be very clear about—and to be able to really articulate—the purpose of each piece in the program. In other words, if you are going to speculate on what curriculum concepts you can connect *to* these pieces, you've got to be very sure about where you are connecting them *from*. Although this sounds incredibly simple and basic, the number of artists who cannot articulate the educational objective of their program is enormous. Once you are able to do this, you are well on your way to discovering connections to other curriculum.

A: But you are suggesting that the artist not attempt to make these connections by themselves.

S: I would suggest strongly that they work with someone from the educational community. They can have some ideas about it, study state or national curriculum standards, and become articulate in discussing these things, but an artist is walking on thin ice going it alone. In any endeavor where you are trying to pass on information and there is a pedagogy of doing it, to think that an artist can in a short time learn this pedagogy really sets them up for being criticized for doing a very superficial job—think about the amount of time that a teacher trains to become a teacher.

A: Do you think it is safe for an artist, without collaborating with an educator, to make very general connections to classroom curriculum? For example, let's say an artist has a program on African dance and knows that the fourth-graders in her state are required to study African history. Would she be safe articulating this connection in her promotional material?

S: Sure.

A: Once developed, are these connections highlighted by the artist during the performance? by the teacher back in the classroom? or both?

S: I think the best way is for it to be done primarily in the classroom. Of course, the artist must understand and use the correct terminology, thus becoming a portal or vehicle through which the teachers see the connections, jump on them, and use them afterwards in the classroom. If you try to make all these connections during the performance, your program can go down so many different paths that you end up compromising your art form.

A: Are there other levels of learning that can be incorporated into an arts performance besides teaching about the art form and making connections to classroom curriculum?

S: The arts help to get kids thinking—even if they don't do it cognitively—about different ways of learning and different ways of knowing. They can take what they learn in this regard and apply it toward other academic areas. For example, in an instrument-building workshop I did in a shop class, the process involved taking abstract plans for percussion instruments, cutting tubes to various lengths, and constructing the instruments. The program is really all about math and science—acoustics, ratios, intervals, cutting and measuring, etc.—but ends up being a performance in the end, when the instruments are actually played. But back to the point about different ways of learning, another thing the kids learned—through the trial and error of measuring, cutting, and adjusting in an attempt to get the instruments to make the sounds we were after—is that things don't always transfer in a precise manner from plans on paper to a finished product. And more importantly, they saw that the result of the precise manufacturing of something, based on a mathematical formula, is often not as pleasing as when you just do it by ear. A child-development psychologist helped me to see this aspect of the program and to see that we are often not even aware of the different ways of learning and teaching that artists have, often unknowingly, incorporated into their programs.

**The Arts-in-Education Institute**

A: Can you tell me what the *Arts-in-Education Institute* program is all about?

S: It's a program that we started in 1989 to begin focusing on professional development for both artists and educators. It started with a five day gathering in upstate New York. We brought together artists, programs directors, and educators from YA chapters all over the country to work on the same kinds of issues we've been talking about here. Then we started having these gatherings in different parts of the country, get-

138

ting the local YA chapters to sponsor them. We had kids involved as well as child-development psychologists.

Today, we conduct these institutes throughout the country. More and more, we're matching educators from various curriculum areas with artists, and we're having them work together in small groups. They work on program design and other areas so that artists are not doing this in a vacuum. Often the educators and artists on a team will be working together in the future through a YA residency program. The teachers are interested in working with the artists in advance in order to maximize the benefits of the residency.

The overall idea of this program is to bring others into the design and implementation process so that artists are not working in a vacuum; that puts them on a pedestal and keeps them there.

# Part Two:
## Interviews, Program Observations and Theme Ideas

The following chapters contain interviews with arts-in-education experts, descriptions of programs I have observed, and ideas for program themes taken from the rosters of various presenting organizations.

The programs I observed were randomly selected. I made no special effort to include cream-of-the-crop programs, although some of them are definitely in that category. While it can be very inspiring for artists just getting started in the schools to see examples of highly sophisticated programs, it can be equally encouraging to see examples of simple, yet effective programs that cause one to say, "Hey, I can do that!" In the six program observations included, you'll find one or two at either end of the spectrum and the rest somewhere in between.

My purpose in observing the programs was not to critique them; therefore, I have not included evaluative comments, only descriptions of what I saw. The main intent is to provide examples of a variety of programs that, in spite of whatever shortcomings they may have, are popular in schools. All of the programs described have been accepted for inclusion on the rosters of one or more presenting organizations.

While there are separate chapters for each of the major disciplines—music, theater, dance, and speaking—I encourage you to read each of the chapters. You will likely discover program-design and presentation ideas that will work equally well in your particular discipline.

It's important to remember that the purpose of these chapters is to prime your brain-storming functions, not to provide an assortment of ready-to-adopt programs. There are no short cuts to the work involved in designing a program. Techniques and ideas that work well for one artist may be ineffective for the next. Creating a program and developing a presentation style that match your unique personality is the only route to a top-quality show.

# CHAPTER 12
# Instrumental Music

For several reasons, developing a program of instrumental music for presentation in schools is challenging. The absence of the use of words, the lack of a significant visual aspect, and the fact that most children have had minimal exposure to instrumental music make these programs more difficult for children to relate to and understand. However, facing these challenges head on, many artists have been extremely successful in developing and presenting instrumental music programs.

The following interview with Dorothy Sasscer of *Chamber Music America* (see Appendix for more information on CMA) addresses the unique situation in which instrumental music finds itself. Dorothy's credentials include serving as Assistant Director of Education with the New York Philharmonic, where she helped develop outreach and education programs, including an educational program for children to support the New York Philharmonic's *Young People's Concerts* series. In her current position as Program Administration Coordinator with CMA, Dorothy assists in coaching emerging artists and ensembles who wish to present programs in schools. Though Dorothy speaks specifically to chamber and classical music, her insights are relevant to all instrumental genres.

*A* indicates the author, *S* indicates Sasscer.

## Program themes

A: During a chamber music presentation for a K-6 audience, what are some educational themes that might be developed?

S: One common theme that classical groups use is to introduce the various instruments as *voices* and help the students hear how those voices interact. Another popular idea is to develop a program that is tied to some curriculum area of the age level the artists are addressing. For example, they'll take music from a certain part of the world and link it to what is already being addressed in the classroom. A common theme is history—the artists will talk about that in terms of folk tunes from particular parts of the world and particular points in history.

A: How important is it that the ensemble offer study guides or follow-up materials to help facilitate the educational objective of the program? Do most ensembles you are aware of do this?

S: That really varies wildly depending on the resources of the particular artists. We strongly encourage artists to work with educators in preparing those materials...with the input of educators you can really make close ties to the curriculum...an educator's view is very different from the artist's view, and there needs to be common ground. Many artists find after completing their education that they may be fine performing musicians but not necessarily fine educators. Many may be clueless as to how to develop a program, speak to students in a way that is not above their comprehension, break things down into digestible segments, know something about managing a group of children, and so forth. Educators can help you with that. You want to keep in mind that children of different ages are learning in different ways. For example, at a certain age they are making comparisons to figure out their place in the universe, so you want to be able to capitalize on that when addressing that particular age group and not ask them to do something that is inappropriate for their development level. Unless you're going to go back to school to learn these things, it's best to work closely with educators as often as you can.

This is especially important if artists want to develop written materials to support their program.

## Audience participation

A: How might audience participation be incorporated into a chamber music presentation?

S: In some of the most successful programs, the ensemble involves the students in identifying rhythmic patterns or melodic themes or following melodies as they move from one instrument to another. Sometimes they have kids sing things back or clap rhythmic patterns. Artists should look into the Orff, Dalcroze and Kod'aly teaching methods for more information on these kinds of student activities. (Author's note: see Appendix for more information).

A: Do ensembles often include demonstrations of how their instruments work and how they produce sound?

S: Absolutely. Introducing a tactile element to your presentation will often elicit enormous response. I'm thinking of a presentation I saw where an oboist and a clarinetist were demonstrating how reeds work using straws and students were engaged in that. Brass players can do presentations using hosing and funnels; string players can use shoe boxes and rubber bands. There are a thousand and one examples. A quick trip to your local library's education shelf should give anyone a ton of ideas.

Artists could also bring in old (not to be used again) reeds, strings, mouthpieces, mutes, combs, mallets—even an instrument—to pass around the room. (While you might be skeptical of how kids will handle these things, you'd be surprised at the respect and care given them—the fact that you've entrusted them with *special things* carries an awful lot of weight.) This gives students a chance to see the tools of your trade *up close and personal*. For kids who have never seen a string, brass, or woodwind instrument, this is very powerful.

145

## Audience management

A: I know, from the hundreds of assemblies I have presented, how important minute-to-minute audience control is. It seems this is a lot easier for an artist such as myself: I have a microphone continually in front of me and can encourage, guide, and manage the audience even between the verses of a song, continuing to play a basic rhythm guitar part. Audience control has to be much more difficult for an instrumentalist who must keep a violin under her chin or reed in her mouth while playing pieces that may be several minutes long. How do the musicians work around this obstacle?

S: The key to that is breaking down the pieces you are going to be performing into digestible segments, appropriate for the age group that you're performing for—younger elementary students have far less attention span than those in grades three through six. Part of the key here is making sure before you go into that piece that you have provided your audience with a focus, whether that is having them raise their hands every time they hear the main melody or clap their hands to a recurring rhythm every time it comes around. Combining active listening with an appropriate length will help keep the children involved. In viewing a series of programs on video tape at a recent conference, in the ones where there was student involvement during the pieces and an opportunity for student response after the pieces, the children were far more well-behaved because their attention was focused on the task at hand.

A: When a lack of attention occurs in the middle of a piece —often because the artists have done something to sabotage themselves—is there anything the artists can do, or are they destined to finish the piece with a distracted audience?

A: That's really hard. I think, like you say, they are doomed to finishing out at least that segment or piece with a distracted audience, although a very flexible and well-rehearsed ensemble could make adjustments *on the fly*.

Instances like the one you describe illustrate why good program structure and advance preparation are so critical to success when presenting programs for children. Should a well-prepared ensemble find their audience becoming fidgety, with a simple gesture they can abbreviate their performance, ending at a predetermined point in the score. If the same thing occurs during a spoken portion of the program, the well-scripted ensemble can insert questions or activities held in reserve for just that reason.

To reach this level of flexibility requires that an ensemble invest time and energy into developing and rehearsing a program that includes the introduction of no more than one or two key musical concepts per 45-minute presentation; performances of an appropriate length for the audience's age-level; a speaking and performing role for *all* members of the ensemble; a concise script using language appropriate to the children's developmental stage; and several alternative components (performances, activities, or questions) held in reserve to *plug in,* if necessary, for the occasional restless audience.

An ensemble should spend at least as much time preparing a children's program as they do an adult one; ideally, they should spend twice as much time. Children are, after all, a less forgiving audience than adults. I can't emphasize enough the importance of advance preparation.

A: Is it important that a member of the ensemble spend a little time at the beginning of the program describing the nature of a chamber performance and how one should conduct oneself at such a performance?

S: No! I mean, I've seen ensembles do that, but I don't think it's helpful. When K-6 kids have the opportunity to ask questions of the artists and to interact with them, you see that they could care less about *what* chamber music is. The composers, the countries they lived in, the century in which they lived—all are meaningless to them. What is important to them is how you learned your instrument, how much do you have to practice, why did you become musicians; to have intelligent answers to those questions encourages them to explore more on their own. Kids at that age are trying to make connections between where you are and where they are: they want to see how they can make the leap to doing what you're doing. The unique character of chamber music is not important to them—I think, meaningless to them; it's like trying to talk about sonata form to a fifth-grader. I don't think talking about what makes your art form different from other art forms (except in a very basic way) really makes any sense until Jr. High or High School.

**Musical content**

A: Given the sophistication of chamber music and the relative lack of musical development of the typical grade school student, how does a chamber ensemble vary the selections enough to keep them from all sounding alike to an elementary student's ears?

S: They can go at it several ways. One, by using pieces with easily identifiable melodies. I watched a woodwind ensemble take Czechoslovakian music heavily based on folk tunes and first play piano arrangements of the pieces so that the kids could sing the tunes. Having set it up this way, the ensemble would play the piece, and the kids could make a connection. Then the next piece they did was Beethoven, which was completely different. Pieces can also be contrasted by differences in range, rhythm, or solo instruments.

Kids up to about 6th grade will listen to almost anything—they're really open, so you have a lot of freedom. I wonder sometimes if ensembles don't restrict themselves unnecessarily, thinking they have to go to *top forty* classical pieces in order to work with kids.

A: Do ensembles sometimes perform their own arrangements of TV show themes, commercials, or things of that nature in order to provide something more familiar for the students?

S: In a K-2 presentation, I watched a jazz ensemble do a jazz version of the *Flintstones Theme,* and the kids were rapt. It went on for five minutes (a long time for that age group!) but it was a tune that they recognized, and they were up and dancing in the auditorium. The artists didn't feel like they had made any great artistic compromises at all. They started with something the kids could get into and later moved to more unfamiliar pieces. If you're relying on the familiar stuff all the time, it's musically unsatisfying for you: you don't want to be playing the *Flintstones* all the time; you want to be playing more challenging pieces. But artists who ignore their audiences doom themselves to failure down the line: there are few people in those audiences anymore who can follow you as you chart out your own musical path, ignoring their knowledge level and familiarity level.

## Technical considerations

A: What would you recommend as the maximum audience size for a chamber music presentation?

S: I know very few ensembles who like to do presentations for very large groups. In fact, I know a great many who actively discourage them. That is not the right environment for chamber ensembles: they're not miked and the sound only goes so far. Most artists ask administrators to try to put together smaller groups where they are dealing with no more than a hundred; a single class of forty or less is really the most ideal. I do know of some artists who do school presentations for larger audiences, and they find them completely unsatisfying. An artist recently told me, to use his words, that he found them to be "the most depressing and discouraging activities" that his ensemble does.

A: For a chamber performance, what in your opinion, is the most effective seating arrangement for students?

S: Most of the time the seating is in the round (or a semi-circle) so the kids can see well from all sides. Many artists are trying to find ways to close the distance between themselves and the audience. Most of them try to avoid being on a stage; intimacy is part of what chamber music is, and they don't want to distance themselves.

## Promotion and booking

A: Have you found that budget cuts in school music programs have actually made it easier for classical artists to find work in schools, as schools try to fill the void in the music curriculum?

S: I wouldn't really say easier, but it has provided more of a market. With a lack of a comprehensive music curriculum in schools, many are using presentations by artists as a means of fulfilling the arts requirement. By having three groups in during the year to do a performance and a series of workshops, one could conceivably satisfy the state music/arts mandates. The administrators are operating out of the mind-set that some exposure is better than none. They can't afford a music specialist in the school, so these performances and workshops are the next best thing their budgets can support.

A: Do most chamber ensembles work with arts commissions, *Young Audiences* or other presenting organizations, or do they often promote and book independent of such support?

S: All of the above. Many artists do work with such organizations, but they also promote and book themselves, pursuing opportunities in the schools on their own. If an ensemble wants an ongoing situation in a school, I encourage them to identify an educator within the school—if they can make a connection with the principle, that's even better—to work with in developing the program. Get the PTA involved; if you can make your case to the parents and teachers, they can often help you establish a relationship with the school, helping you find your way in on a regular basis.

## PROGRAM OBSERVATIONS

### Wind quintet

After being introduced by the principal, the ensemble, starting from the back of the room, proceeds up the side and center aisles, surrounding the audience with music. Upon arriving at the front of the room, the musicians line up side by side, continuing the piece and getting the audience to clap along. At the end of the piece, they thank the kids for joining in clapping and tell them there will be no other places in the program where the kids should clap along or make any noise except to applaud at the end of the selections.

In the next segment, a member of the ensemble explains that, during the show, students will learn how music is used as communication—how pitch, rhythm, melody, and harmony set moods and creates feelings. To demonstrate this concept, the oboist plays a haunting tune while a puppet depicting a snake appears, slithering around the oboe. Next, the bassoonist plays the theme of the *Alfred Hitchcock Show* to illustrate how music can depict mystery.

Following an up-tempo classical number, the ensemble demonstrates how horns were used in ancient times to communicate. As horn calls are passed back and forth, the clarinetist hams it up by putting his instrument to his ear as he listens to responses.

In the next segment, to demonstrate how music builds suspense, a member of the ensemble comes out in a brim hat, playing the role of an emcee at a state-fair stadium show. He announces that there will be a great spectacle of two trains approaching one another on the same track. With speakers strategically placed at either side of the stage, a stereo sound track plays train horns while the ensemble begins the next piece. At first, the horn blasts sound far away and faint, and the music is subdued. But as the blasts become louder and

151

more frequent, the ensemble's music becomes more and more frenzied and frantic, building the suspense that climaxes at the end of the number.

In the next segment—a demonstration of the operational principals of a flute—a piece is performed using tubes of varying lengths swung overhead. Each tube can sound different notes, depending on how fast it is swung through the air. The artists create haunting melodies and harmonies by carefully orchestrating the movement of the tubes.

Next is a number from the movie, *Star Wars*. After a tongue-in-cheek introduction of the *Cantina Band,* the ensemble, decked out in outer-space masks, demonstrates how a buoyant party feeling can be created through music. Kazoos and other zany instruments are featured in the skit.

In the grand finale, *Peter and the Wolf*, the kids see how the nature of the melodies and the timbre of the instruments portray characters in the story. To help the audience distinguish the characters, the flute player wears a colored hat with a feather, the oboe player wears a duck hat, the clarinet player wears a cat mask and hat that says *CAT* (the logo of a heavy-equipment manufacturer), and the horn player wears a hand puppet depicting a wolf. Members of the ensemble take turns narrating the story in theatrical voices while the musicians pantomime their roles as they play their instruments: the horn player (the wolf) rushes at the duck and the bird, blasting his horn in a threatening manner, the clarinetist (the cat) sneaks and slinks around, the flutist (the bird) flits lightly about the stage, the oboist (the duck) waddles slowly about. To emphasize key parts of the narrative, the ensemble recites the lines in unison. Instruments are used in theatrical ways during the story: the clarinet is pulled in two and used to depict binoculars, the oboe is brought up to the eye as a rifle, etc. Students see how the sounds and melodies create moods and identities for the various roles.

## Jazz trio

This trio consists of a mallet player (vibraphone & xylophone), an electric bassist, and a drummer. The trio opens the show with an up-tempo number, foregoing any verbal introduction.

Following the first number, a member of the ensemble discusses the history and improvisatory nature of jazz. He describes *Mallet Jazz* as jazz that is played on instruments struck with a mallet, explaining a little about the instruments themselves.

In the next segment, the mallet player discusses the Swing era and Lionel Hampton's role in it. He tells the story of how Hampton, never having seen a vibraphone before, came across one in the back corner of a recording studio. Someone in the studio explained to Hampton that the instrument was used in sound tracks of science-fiction movies. (The mallet player demonstrates some typical sound effects.) Hampton decided the instrument would work nicely for Jazz and soon the whole world was listening to Hampton and his new instrument. Wrapping up the narrative, the drummer announces, to the oohs and aahs of the kids, that the next song is the theme song from *The Pink Panther*.

The next segment focuses on the Bee-Bop era. The segment begins with a brief discussion of the era and ends with the performance of a another audience favorite—a character theme from the *Peanuts* cartoon.

In the next segment, which illustrates the nature of improvisation, the mallet player selects a student to come forward and play the xylophone. Limiting the student to two keys on the instrument, he shows the student how to strike the keys and explains that the student's task is to do a short, five-or-six-strike improvisation every time there is a break in the music. He assures the student that this improvisation will work out perfectly every time. The band breaks every few bars and the student strikes the keys a little differently each time. Indeed, it works out perfectly every time, and the crowd loves it.

Following a session of Q&A, the trio closes with a tune from the *Big Band* era.

## OTHER PROGRAM IDEAS

**Brass quintet:** Each instrument of the brass family is individually introduced, followed by a piece featuring a solo by the the just-introduced instrument. The musical selections cover everything from important classical compositions to cartoon themes. Special sections provide information on how brass instruments have been used in the past for hunting calls and even for telling time. Students participate by conducting the ensemble and assisting in demonstrations illustrating the working mechanics of the instruments. One demonstration involves the construction of an instrument using a mouthpiece and bell connected by a garden hose.

**Solo violin:** Featuring violin pieces from around the world, the artist covers everything from Irish, Appalachian, and Israeli folk tunes to Bach and Brahms. Historical, cultural, and ethnic background information is provided for each piece, linking the music to history and other curriculum areas. A blazing old-time fiddle number is a real show stopper.

**Solo Cello:** This program features both the traditional acoustic cello and the more modern electric cello. Highlights of the program include a segment on the use of cellos in movie and television scores, a demonstration of how the cello can play popular music as well as classical, and a segment featuring ethnic cello music from around the world.

**Synthesizer:** This program is designed to show how the use of computer technology has affected the way in which sounds and music can be created. The technique of *sampling* instruments in order to duplicate their sounds electronically is covered as well as how the synthesizer can create totally new sounds.

**African drums (solo artist):** Students participate in authentic African dances and drumming. The role of drumming in African traditions is discussed. How participation in joyful songs, stories and dance encourages children to love and respect one another is explored. In a demonstration, students learn how to make African-style drums at home.

**Traditional instruments (solo artist):** The artist presents traditional instruments and music of many countries and cultures, demonstrating the sounds of recorders, marimbas, harps, drums, etc. The social roles of both music and musicians in various cultures is explored throughout the program. Students are involved in both the making and playing of simple traditional instruments.

**Violin and piano:** This program is an exploration of the repertoire of solo violin accompanied by piano. The artists perform selections that tell stories, describe scenes, or create moods. A segment of international music covers everything from American folk music to German chamber music. The role of violin and piano music in dance and theater is covered as well.

**Authentic South American instruments** are the focus of this program presented by an instrumental duo. Instruments featured include the following: hand-carved Indian flutes, bamboo pan pipes, turtle shell, goat feet, rain stick, tiple, and charango—a ten-string instrument originally made with an armadillo shell. Details are provided about how the instruments are made and played, including a demonstration showing how pan pipes can be readily made from PVC pipe.

**Performing Bach and playing baseball** are shown to be similar activities in a program presented by a woodwind quintet. The ensemble explores the concepts of sportsmanship, getting along with others, teamwork, appreciation for differences, and coordination, showing how these concepts lead to success—both on the field and in the recital hall.

# CHAPTER 13
# Theater

Because theater is both visual and verbal in nature and because the performance pieces have a storytelling nature, the art form is very accessible to children. The verbal aspect of theater also makes possible the development of programs with non-art themes or ethnic themes in addition to themes that develop concepts relating to the art form itself.

In many theater programs, the emphasis is on performance: the artists perform a single story or play (or series of stories or plays) with little or no narrative, demonstrations or other segments of non-performance content. The works presented in these performance-orientated programs range from classic children's works such as *Hiawatha, Sleeping Beauty,* and *Aladdin* to the artist's original creations. Other theater programs consist of several shorter performance pieces woven together with narrative, demonstrations, and activities. These programs often develop themes about the elements, history, styles, production, or other aspects of the art form.

## PROGRAM OBSERVATIONS

### African marionettes

Dressed in colorful, authentic West African clothing, the performers enter the auditorium through a back door and make an ceremonial procession to the stage, accompanied by the driving rhythm of a drum. In the procession there are two marionettes—a bigger-than-life antelope and a man over eight feet tall—and a dancer playing rhythm instruments as she dances. The commotion of sights, sounds, and movement immediately command the students' attention. After arriving on a stage decorated with colorful backdrops, the performers continue their drumming and dancing for another moment or two.

Without further ado, the drummer initiates a conversation with the antelope, reminding him that today is the day of the *great festival* and inquiring as to whether the antelope is ready to perform. After some prodding, the antelope indicates that he indeed remembers that the festival is today and that he is ready for the show. The drumming resumes, and the antelope begins spinning around and around, turning faster and faster until he is rotating like a top. As the tempo increases, the dancer gets the kids clapping along to the infectious rhythm of the drumming.

The next segment begins with a narrative about the ensemble's particular style of puppetry, how African puppet festivals bring villagers together, and the role of the audience in the festival performances. The drummer then teaches the kids a call-and-response song. There are only minor differences between his part and theirs, so it is a little confusing for the kids at first. He has some fun with the kids helping them get the parts straight. Once everyone is ready to go, he resumes the beating of the drum and begins the song. The room is immediately energized with pounding rhythm, chanting, and clapping. In the meantime, the antelope is transformed into a puppet stage. Two puppets begin dancing on the stage as the drumming and chanting fade.

The dancer introduces the first story, which is based on various inanimate objects (potatoes, shirts, trees, etc.) coming to life and talking with the puppets. As successive characters try to tell the others about the strange occurrences they saw, no one believes them. The puppets often ask the audience *yes-no* questions and other questions with obvious answers, which the kids answer in unison. The story is accompanied by drums and authentic African instruments.

As the first story ends, the dancer takes the stage while the puppeteers get set for the next story—a tale about a boogey man who hides his identity in order to get married. The boogey man initiates a dialogue with the dancer, explaining all the things he finds ugly about himself and how beautiful he would be if only he could fix these things. He drops behind the puppet stage several times, each time reappearing with the suggested modifications: new teeth, eyes, nose, etc. He engages the audience in letting him know if he has the new feature in the right place on his face and the extent to which the feature improves his looks. At the end of the story, the kids join in singing an African song that has served as the musical theme for the show.

As the stage is rearranged for the final story, the eight-foot-tall puppet comes out and performs a dance. The final story is about a chicken who convinces an alligator that she is the alligator's sister in order to spare herself being eaten by the alligator. At the end of the story, the alligator—a huge green puppet—comes out for a dance and charges the kids in the front row with his mouth wide open as though he were going to eat them. The audience squeals with delight. Eventually, the antelope and the rest of the ensemble join the alligator in this final dance.

In the last segment, the puppeteers appear, take questions, and demonstrate the workings of each of the puppets.

## Mask theater

This program consists of several five- or six- minute pieces performed by artists wearing masks. The pieces are accompanied by an assortment of instruments that includes an unusual, bowed instrument, a synthesizer, a flute, an electronic drum, and a guitar. The instruments are used in setting the tone and mood for each of the pieces. With the exception of one piece, there is no dialogue—the performances are mimed.

The program begins with the accompanist asking questions of the audience as a whole: Do they like chocolate? How many people want to be firemen when the grow up? How many don't want to grow up at all?... The kids respond enthusiastically.

Moving into the next segment, the accompanist briefly describes what the kids will see in the course of the program. He explains that each skit will begin with actors coming through the stage curtain and end when the actors go back behind the curtain. He goes on to explain that when the actors exit the stage through the curtain, the audience should applaud.

In the first skit, two actors wearing masks and facing outward at either end of a long, flexible tube come out from behind the curtain. Upon discovering they are connected by the tube, they endeavor to separate themselves from one another. They eventually succeed in splitting into two smaller tubes. Following a celebration of their success, they come back together again, but this time as a voluntary union of two separate entities.

As the actors prepare for the next piece, the musician takes the stage, racing back and forth with an electronic drum. The drum beats on its own, mystifying the musician. Whenever the musician strikes the drum himself, the drum echoes back the pattern he plays, further confounding him. This theme escalates without resolution until the actors are ready for the next performance.

The next skit is entitled *The Autograph*. When an elderly couple come upon a movie star—humorously portrayed by a cross-dressed male actor—they ask her for an autograph. The movie star signs a slip of paper offered by the old woman, but rushes off as the old man attempts to get an autograph for himself. The old woman—seeing his disappointment—gives the autograph to her husband in a gesture of kindness. After looking it over and pondering the matter for a moment, the man tears the autograph in two, giving half the slip of paper back to the woman. They look at one another, smile, and walk off hand in hand. Punctuating the moral of the story, a first-grader exclaims happily, "They both get to have half."

The next skit features two men wearing similar masks. Coming from behind the curtain, one man is crawling on all fours while the other, holding a long rod, rides standing on his back. Reaching center stage, the man with the rod gets off the other's back, while the man upon whom he was riding lays over on the floor. In a moment, the man with the rod, ready to ride again, pokes the other with the rod in an attempt to get him back up off the floor. Though he is hurt by the rod, the man on the floor struggles to get up. Then suddenly the man with the rod seems to recognize him as a human being for the first time; he tosses the rod to the side, and helps the man on the floor to his feet. Arm in arm, they begin leaving the stage. Just before they reach the curtain, the man who has given up the rod looks back to where it lies on the stage. Someone in the audience says, "The stick, the stick...get the stick." The man slowly turns his eyes to the audience, then back to the stick. Contemplating the situation for a moment, he turns once again to the audience and shakes his head "no."

Before the ensemble closes with a segment of Q&A, three actors dressed as clowns perform an improvisational piece, each wearing what is introduced as "the smallest mask in the world"—a red clown's nose. The improvisation takes place on a park bench and involves numerous clown-type antics.

## OTHER PROGRAM IDEAS

**Mime show:** Broadening the definition of mime theater, this program combines classical mime technique, old-world clowning, magic, juggling, music, and improvisation. Musical accompaniment ranges from ragtime to rock. Audience participants are involved in many of the pieces. Students learn to create and respond to a world of illusion in empty space.

**Single actor performing Shakespeare:** Breaking down the language barrier that often exists between younger students and Shakespeare, the actor focuses on the situations faced by Romeo, Juliet, Kate, Petruchio, Macbeth and other Shakespearian characters. Each segment draws connections between the situation in the play and situations students face in every-day life. The program fosters an interest in Shakespeare and inspires creative thinking.

**Dr. Martin Luther King's speeches** comprise the repertoire of this artist. Having received permission from Yolanda King, Director of the Martin Luther King, Jr. Center for Non-Violent Social Change, to portray her father professionally, the artist visits schools, reciting one of four famous King speeches as the content of the program. Discussion and Q&A with the audience follow the performance.

**Historic African-Americans:** Portrayals of prominent Civil War Era civil-rights leaders—Harriet Tubman, Sojourner Truth, and Frederick Douglass—comprise the program content. The program has ties to New York State History and U.S. History. Also very appropriate for Black History Month.

**Bunraku puppetry:** The ensemble uses three distinct types of life-sized puppets—rod, hand, and full body—to bring a Japanese style of puppetry called Bunraku to life. Program content consists of short skits, combining pantomime with slapstick comedy. After the program, the artists demonstrate how the puppets work and field questions from the audience.

**Native American stories:** Creating a visualization of the context in which Native American stories were told, this program consists of stories that bring to life the rich storytelling tradition of local tribes. Covering all facets of early Native American life, the program ties into the history curriculum.

**Tales from the East** combines mask, mime, storytelling, and music to present folk tales from Japan, China, Australia, and other countries. Between the stories are segments dealing with the elements and techniques of storytelling.

**A montage of stories**, ranging from old folk tales to new original tales make up the content of a program presented by a storyteller. Story topics include dinosaurs, girls with ten-foot-long names, bubble gum, best friends, baby gorillas, friendly monsters, and the common cold. Autoharp accompaniment heightens the action in the stories. Between stories, the artist often performs a short piece on spoons or jaw harp. Audience participation in the stories is a distinctive feature of the program.

# CHAPTER 14
# Dance

Dance artists have several options for program themes. Many dance programs presented in schools develop arts-education themes that focus on the elements, history, styles, or creation of dance. For artists who specialize in folk dancing, the development of programs with ethnic themes is an additional option. In programs with ethnic themes, there is considerable opportunity for making connections to non-art curriculum areas such as history and social studies.

## PROGRAM OBSERVATIONS

### Classical music and modern dance

Introducing the program, a dancer acting as emcee explains to the audience that although there will be no narration or breaks in the show, the show is not all one piece—that the pieces are not connected in any way, nor do they comprise any sort of story or play. She asks the students to watch for the overall visual image that each piece creates and to try to retain that image in their minds.

In the first piece, six dancers dressed in leotards and shorts take to the gym floor, dancing to prerecorded classical music played through a PA system. Elements of ballet are combined with modern dance movements. Some of the movements are humorous portrayals of everyday motions such as walking, skipping, and running. The humor helps keep the audience engaged.

The next number features many jumps, lifts, and catches, which really impress the kids. Several solo and duet segments are featured during this piece.

The next segment begins with two dancers, each with a deck of playing cards, sitting at separate desks. Eyeballing one another, they begin shuffling the cards and banging them loudly against the table as they straighten the deck after each shuffle. Having set a slapstick tone, they begin building card houses in a competitive spirit. One is very good at it, the other hopeless. The hopeless one keeps looking at the other in a frustrated effort to figure out how she keeps the cards from continually collapsing. Finally, reaching a peak of frustration, the hopeless one walks over to the talented one, watches her for a moment, and then knocks the card house—now a veritable mansion—to the floor. In the ensuing chase, a new dancer appears, gathers the cards, curiously looks them over for a moment, throws them into the air, and begins the next dance, which is full of slides, jumps, and other acrobatics.

Before the next piece, a dancer in a long, flowing gown appears. A second dancer is hidden underneath the train of the gown. The dancer in the gown begins putting on lipstick, trying to act well-bred and sophisticated. Meanwhile, the one under the train is creating all sorts of commotion with the skirt, flipping it into the air and whipping it about. Finally, the dancer in the gown haughtily flings up her gown, revealing the trouble maker, who is now left sitting exposed on the floor. The audience roars as she strikes an I-wasn't-doing-anything pose.

Next is a dance involving lots of synchronized and mirrored movements, including a segment depicting gossip being passed from one dancer to another. The last dancer in the gossip succession punctuates the end of segment with a flabbergasted look directed at the audience.

In the final piece, all the dancers are dressed in long flowing skirts (later said to be made out of old parachutes). The musical selection is a soft, slow, pipe organ piece. The skirts are billowed, draped, twirled, and puffed, creating a kaleidoscope of images. Combined with the elegant music, the graceful processions and formations represent a real contrast to the previous pieces. In an inspired climax, a huge skirt is sent aloft, slowly descending and coming down over all the dancers. The audience is rapt as a single dancer emerges through an opening in the center of the drape and performs a solo dance.

Following the program, each dancer introduces herself, tells about her background in dance, and fields a question or two from the audience.

## African music and dance

The curtains come up, revealing three young women dressed in authentic African clothing, sitting on chairs. Drums, a drummer, and other instruments are in the background. Responding to the effective staging, a little girl in the front row comments with delight, "Ooooh! African girls." The leader of the ensemble warms the audience up by getting them to respond "Good Morning!" in an enthusiastic manner and tells them it will be okay for them to respond verbally throughout the program. She explains that in Africa the audience is always part of the performance. Continuing in this vein, she tells the kids she believes that if you can talk, you can sing, and if you can walk, you can dance. She asks the kids if they agree, and they all respond in unison, "Yes!"

The first piece is comprised of solo vocal improvisation over a continuous refrain sung in three-part harmony. The song is accompanied by an instrument identified as a mbira. Before the piece begins, one of the musicians briefly describes and demonstrates the instrument.

165

Without pausing, the ensemble leader moves into the next piece—an African folk tale. She has the kids repeat some African words and phrases, adding rhythm and melody as they catch on. Explaining that, in the story, the audience will be singing the theme song, she selects volunteers to come up and learn some dance steps to go with the song. She demonstrates the song and the dance and gets the volunteers dancing while the audience claps and sings. As their confidence builds, she begins a vocal improvisation. With everyone now rehearsed and ready to go, she tells the kids the story behind the next song: Because animals have been eating the family's corn, family members are going to take turns guarding it. First a boy tries, then his mother, then his father. But each time, the animals distract them by singing and dancing, knowing that humans, unable to resist the temptation to sing and dance, will join in and forget all about protecting the corn. As the story unfolds, the ensemble leader humorously depicts each of the family members being drawn into the singing and dancing.

As the volunteers make their way back to their seats, two drummers begin a call-and-response number. There is no verbal introduction or explanation to the piece, but there's a definite implication that communication is taking place through the drumming. The rhythm and intensity of the drumming build as the piece progresses. A brief demonstration of how African drums are constructed follows the piece. During the segment, a student is called forward to assist in stretching and tightening a skin over the hollow body of a drum.

Next, thirty student volunteers are selected for a line dance. Once they are assembled up front, the ensemble leader introduces a new instrument, the marimba, and explains that three marimbas will be used during the piece. As the ensemble begins playing, she gets the audience clapping along while she teaches the volunteers several steps to the dance. During the performance of the piece, she leads the volunteers in the dance steps while she does a vocal improvisation over the ensemble's playing and singing.

Before the last piece, which is performed by a trio of dancers, the leader introduces the members of the ensemble.

At the end of the program, the leader asks the kids to name each of the instruments she has introduced during the course of the show. After this, students are invited to ask questions of the ensemble.

## OTHER PROGRAM IDEAS

**Dance duo:** The relationship between dance and everyday movement is the theme of the program. The artists create and perform dances based on movements such as walking, jumping, skipping and gesturing. One program segment demonstrates how modifying the elements of dance in a handshake change the meaning and feeling communicated in the gesture. Remaining in their seats, students explore the function of various elements of dance through hand movements. Students learn the vocabulary of dance throughout the program.

**Mexican folk dancing:** Broadening awareness and appreciation for Mexican culture, the program introduces students to the dance, music, and customs of Mexico. Connections are drawn between Mexican folk dance and history. Students learn how to speak several words in Spanish. The program is designed to build pride among Hispanic youth.

**How to create a dance** is the theme of a program presented by a six-member dance company. The program consists of several contrasting modern-dance sections interspersed with discussions, demonstrations, and audience participation. Elements of choreographic tools such as unison, counterpoint, canon, accumulation, theme and variation, partnering, and the use of music are explained and demonstrated. Through showing students how the elements are employed in building a dance, the program inspires students with new creative ideas and demonstrates that discipline and abstraction can be fun.

167

# CHAPTER 15
# Singers

Singers have perhaps more options regarding theme and content of their programs than artists of any other discipline or genre. In addition to the typical arts-education themes, the presence of words in songs allows for the ready development of non-art educational themes. Popular non-art themes include environmental responsibility, good citizenship, non-violent problem solving, and avoiding drug abuse. Also, ethnic themes can be developed in programs of songs from specific countries, regions, and peoples—appalachian folk songs, Native American songs, Hispanic songs, etc. In addition, singers can utilize songs as a medium to educate students about the meaning and significance of holidays, centennial and bicentennial celebrations, and other historical events.

## PROGRAM DESCRIPTIONS

**Latin American music ensemble:** Taking the audience on an imaginary tour, visiting the countries of Central America, South America and the Caribbean, this program addresses not only the music of these areas, but the culture and history of the peoples as well. A significant visual aspect is created by the use of large maps, globes, and national flags that move across the stage during the performances. As an introduction to many of the areas *visited* through a song, students are involved in playing a game or participating in a dance native to the country or area in which the song originates. Narratives and demonstrations show how the music of each country in the region has affected the music of the others. Latin American music's influence on rock is also explored.

**Active citizenship** is the theme of a program presented by a guitar and vocal folk duo. Students are encouraged to become involved in recycling, non-violent problem solving, preventing substance abuse, and other activities, helping to make the world a better, safer place for all. Program content consists of topical songs woven together by narratives, stories, and skits. The incorporation of American Sign Language on several songs serves to keep the audience focused and engaged.

**The history of pop music** from the 50's to the 80's is covered in program presented by a four-member ensemble. The program draws connections between music and political, social, and cultural events. Students learn about history through songs of the Kennedy years, the Civil Rights Movement, the Viet Nam War, Watergate, and the Reagan years. Designed for upper elementary-level students.

**An operatic tenor** has developed a program with musical content that ranges from the music of Mozart to Broadway's greatest hits. The elements of musical theater and their use in such productions as *The Phantom of the Opera* comprise a sub-theme of the program.

**Traditional American folk music** is the theme of a program presented by a solo vocalist accompanying himself on a variety of traditional folk instruments including mandolin, guitar, banjo, and dulcimer. Musical content includes Anglo-Saxon ballads, party songs, fiddle tunes, gospel songs, bluegrass, and ragtime. Connections are drawn between the songs and such historical events as the Emancipation Proclamation, the development of railroads, and the European and African immigration.

169

**A joyful appreciation of our diversity** is the objective of a program presented by a singer/guitarist and a sign language interpreter. Songs, stories, and sing-alongs provide students with insights into the lives of those who face unique challenges in movement and communication. Students participate in sign language throughout the program. Connections are made between the theme and health, foreign language, social studies, and music curriculums.

**Renaissance singers** have a program designed to enhance students' interest in singing and encourage participation in school music programs. The sixteen vocalists perform everything from early madrigals, which feature a variety of solos and duets, to Broadway tunes and folk songs. Singing techniques such as posture and breathing are demonstrated, as well as conducting techniques. Students participate in warm-up exercises and are given an opportunity to conduct the ensemble.

**Black American music** is the focus of a program presented by a solo blues artist. Combining recordings of blues artists with live performance, the artist traces the evolution of blues music from the African influence through the modern blues music of today. The use of the harmonica, animal sounds, and train sounds in blues music are explored. Demonstrations include examples of other black American music traditions such as zydeco and the ring shout. The artist shows the blues to be a valid art form and perhaps the most influential music of the 20th century.

**Opera:** In a program designed to demonstrate that an opera is simply a play or story that is sung, the ensemble shows how the singing voice adds emotion and defines characters. In addition, students learn how characters use costumes and props to create drama. Audience members are involved in on-stage musical conversations, scenes, and improvisations.

# CHAPTER 16
# Speakers

Speakers are typically booked in schools to present programs addressing social issues students face in their daily lives. Speakers are also often called on to provide motivational programs to inspire kids to better themselves and to realize their full potential.

The following interview was granted by Micky Fisher. Micky is founder and director of Jostens Speakers Bureau. For twelve years, Jostens has served the educational market, providing speakers for school assembly programs, as well as workshops and in-service programs for teachers and administrators. In 1994 Micky served a term as co-chair of the National Speakers Association's Professional Emphasis Group. (See the Appendix for contact information on Jostens Speakers Bureau and the National Speakers Association.)

*A* indicates the author. *F* indicates Fisher.

## Program topics

A: What topics are schools most interested in having speakers address?

F: A popular topic at the elementary-school level is accepting differences—either disabilities or cultural differences. Our speakers who have physical challenges are often asked to go to

171

elementary schools. In addressing cultural differences, many elementary schools will have an *Awareness Day* for different cultures, and they might ask for a Latino speaker or a black speaker.

The most requested topics at the junior high and high school level, beyond basic youth motivation, are the heavy issues: substance abuse, crime, violence, AIDS—all the prevention issues. Also, character development, values, and responsible decision-making are emerging as new issues for speakers.

A: Are speakers much in demand for holidays such as Veterans Day, Martin Luther King Day, Presidents Day, and other national holidays?

F: Probably the number one demand is speakers for Red Ribbon Week—a national drug-prevention week. Number two would be Black History Month. Then there might be themes within schools like *Diversity Week* or *Wellness Week,* and the school will want a presentation to tie in. We're also asked for presentations with election themes: many schools will have an *election convention* in the spring before they hold student-body elections.

A: Are costume portrayals effective for holiday occasions?

F: I know they're out there, and I understand they do great work, but I've never been asked to book one through the bureau. These might be more popular in elementary schools, but I have not seen them in junior high schools or high schools.

A: In an elementary school, there is a great deal of difference in the emotional and intellectual development of a first-grader and that of a sixth-grader. How does a speaker make sure his program content is accessible to all?

F: If the content of the speech is entertainment orientated it has a better chance of being appropriate for all. However, if the content deals with heavier subject matter, the student body must be broken down into age groups so that the content can be made appropriate for each age group.

A: Is it necessary for a speaker to have personal experience with the topic she is addressing in order to be effective? For example, does a speaker addressing the issue of drug abuse have to be a former user.

F: Twelve years ago, when a school wanted a presentation on substance abuse, they wanted a speaker who had never used. Now many clients prefer to have a speaker who has been through recovery.

There are many speakers who have never abused alcohol or drugs, and they do wonderful presentations. They are well-educated on the topic of substance abuse and thoroughly understand young people and the challenges they face. As skilled speaking professionals, they avoid being self-righteous or scolding. Instead, they offer guidance and hope to those in need—and support those already making responsible choices.

Former alcohol and drug users, active in recovery, can also be very powerful. They bring unique credibility and offer empowerment to those students in trouble or on the edge. In order for these speakers to be meaningful role models, it is vital that they have years of recovery behind them and have profound wisdom to share. If the years of recovery are not in place, there is a chance the speaker's personal issues might be too raw to share with young people. They must be educated, talented, and very genuine in their concern for young people.

Thus, it is the speaker's education, communication skills, depth of wisdom from personal experience, talent, and attitude that affect the true value of the speaker's message. Both former substance abusers and those who have never abused can be highly effective speakers. If the speaker is genuine in his concern for young people—and all the above points are in place—the audience will listen and learn.

A: Some of the issues speakers address—drugs, alcohol, gangs, violence—must hit pretty close to home for many students.

How does a speaker prepare herself to deal with a situation where students may react to the program content in a very emotional way?

F: There are certain speakers I am uncomfortable working with: those that really feel empowered by encouraging students to express their emotions. I've had speakers tell me, "Oh, you should see me—I can make every kid cry—it's just wonderful." That attitude concerns me. Then there are speakers who have students come up and share a personal challenge. That's not appropriate because they could say something negative about their family or peers in a public setting. It's only natural for some emotions to be touched during a speech, but the speaker should not pressure the audience for response.

When a speaker knows that their topic is likely to cause a reaction in some students, it is vital that they prepare the school staff before the event and offer meaningful follow-up. For example, I have speakers who portray characters in abusive families. Some students might see their mom or dad in the portrayal and think, "Oh! Now I understand why my dad acts that way. Maybe he's an alcoholic." For such programs, it is beneficial to advise the counseling department and teaching staff prior to the program so that they can be prepared and be receptive to students who want to talk.

Toward the end of the speech, these speakers might plan for follow-up support in several ways: make themselves available after the program to talk with those wanting advice; arrange for counselors to be available to meet with students; leave behind pamphlets with supportive information, a list names and phone numbers of local organizations or professionals who can provide assistance, and a list of books that may be helpful. Some speakers even make themselves available through the Internet to answer students' questions.

For speakers who address the tough issues, it is critical to focus on solutions and inform students how and where to find help. Don't ever leave young people hanging with nowhere to go.

## Pre-planning

A: What actions should a speaker encourage the school to take in helping ensure a successful presentation?

F: It's important that the speaker be seen from head to toe during the presentation: if all the students see is the top of the speaker's head moving around, they are not going to be as attentive. The students should be seated close to the stage area, and all the seats up front should be filled. The temperature of the room needs to be comfortable. The school needs to provide the best possible sound system they can get their hands on. If they don't have a good system, they need to be encouraged to borrow or rent one, because the sound is absolutely critical to the success of the program. (I have seen speakers handed a megaphone or a box-type microphone with a six-foot cord—that's not going to work.) It's important that a school administrator or teacher quiet the audience and then introduce the speaker. Teachers should stay in the room during the assembly so that if there are any disturbances the teacher can take care of it, not the speaker.

## Presentation

A: What are some effective methods speakers use to get the students' attention right away?

F: Speakers have many different ways of doing this—humor, personal stories, etc. The main thing is that the speaker needs to realize that once they take the microphone, it's show time. They are not a classroom teacher; they are a special presenter with presentation skills that are far more animated and dramatic than a classroom situation calls for. If they start off in a *classroom* mode and there is not much theater, the audience is going to have a hard time tuning in.

A: Is it important that the speaker get off the platform and out into the audience?

# Jostens *Top 10 Tips* for assembly coordinators

**1. Scheduling: Morning assemblies generate more excitement than those in the afternoon.** Assemblies scheduled too close to lunch hour can lead to restlessness.

**2. Timing: Most speakers require between 45 and 60 minutes.** Allow additional time for seating, announcements, etc. Silence the bells during the program.

**3. Venue: A theater or auditorium is best.** A gymnasium will work only if the audience is seated on one side facing the speaker! If there are more students than will fit on the bleachers on one side, seat remaining students on floor or in chairs.

**4. Staging: Most speakers don't use a podium.** So keep the stage free and clear, allowing plenty of room for freedom of movement. The microphone is positioned free-standing with enough cord to permit the speaker to cover the full width of the venue. The audience should be as close to the stage as possible.

**5. Sound: If the speaker cannot be heard clearly by everyone in the assembly, the program is "doomed" before it starts.** If your school does not have a quality sound system (quality microphone, quality amplifier, and quality speakers) buy, rent, or borrow...just make sure the speaker has this vital tool.

**6. Lights: Students get *ancy* if they cannot see what is happening.** Make certain that the speaker is fully lit so the audience can see facial expressions and gestures, props, chalkboards, etc...

**7. Atmosphere: Ambience sets the mood and tone for the assembly.** Attention spans will easily evaporate in a hot, stuffy room. Keep the room at a comfortable temperature, adjusted for the size of the crowd. A positive climate is further insured when music (popular rock) is played as the students enter the venue.

**8. Seating: To every great assembly, there is a sense of order.** Instead of *open seating* (which can often be chaotic and disruptive) teachers should arrive with their respective class and sit among them in a preassigned section. This way, each teacher takes responsibility for the appropriate behavior of their students.

**9. Introduction: The introduction is a critical part of the performance.** It builds credibility for the speaker and peaks the interest of the audience. The introduction should begin only after the audience is seated and the room is quiet. Most speakers use their introduction to *set up* their talk and prefer it to be read verbatim.

**10. Conclusion: The speaker should not have to dismiss the students.** This task, and any other beyond the program itself, should be handled by a teacher or an administrator.

Figure 16-1: A list of reminders created by Jostens and sent to assembly coordinators prior to a speaker's appearance.

F: If speakers are going to go out into the audience and work the crowd, they need to be extremely spontaneous. It's risky business: it can backfire if the speaker is not skilled in handling various audience reactions. It's certainly not a necessity.

A: You've been quoted as saying, "The best programs put the kids on a roller coaster ride, laughing one minute and quiet and intense the next." Can you expand on this a little?

F: I think of a speakers as performers with many facets. In order to hold a young audience's attention, speakers will change their pacing: they might at first be very animated and then still and dramatic, or they might be high-energy for awhile and then low-keyed. Young people's attention span can be very short, and so putting dynamics and theatrics into the program helps the audience stay tuned because they don't know what's around the next corner. If a speaker just stays in one mode for forty-five minutes she's going to lose her audience.

A: Are personal stories effective in getting a message across?

F: Definitely. Especially if the speaker is serving as a role model, young people are very empowered by their personal stories: maybe they see where the speaker struggled or lived in a poor family and yet still went to college.

A: Should speakers simply speak, or should they develop ways to involve the audience (or individual members of the audience) in the program?

F: If the speaker is doing his job the audience is already involved through intensely active listening. If it's a workshop, then there is likely to be more interaction between the speaker and the audience.

A: Generally, speakers welcome ongoing response from the audience: laughter, gasps, cheering, etc. What techniques can be employed to keep these responses within certain limits—to keep the audience's response under control so that it does not impede the forward movement of the program?

F: What works is to allow an appropriate amount of time for the emotion to be expressed and then continue in a calm voice and just keep going. If the speaker has engaged the audience, they'll want to hear what he has to say next, and they will quiet down.

A: What are some effective techniques for restoring order and regaining attention if the audience gets rowdy?

F: The speaker can stop, look down, pace a little bit, wait—let their body language say, "Okay, I'll give you some time." If that doesn't work, they may need to walk over and make eye contact with the group of students causing the disturbance. I've heard speakers tell kids that if they are not interested in the program, it would be okay if they left now so others can listen. Most likely these students will then quiet down. By doing these sorts of things, you avoid repeatedly asking the audience to be quiet, but at the same time you're setting some boundaries.

A: What are some effective techniques for soliciting questions from the audience? Should students come forward and use a microphone? If not, how can the speaker insure that both she and the audience can hear the question?

F: If the student can't get to a microphone, it's important that the speaker repeat the question over the microphone for the audience. When the program includes several minutes of Q&A at the end, I've seen some speakers have a second microphone placed in a side aisle or in the back of the room. That way students with questions can form a line behind the microphone and use it when it's their turn to ask a question. Just make sure that one way or the other the question gets over a microphone.

**Technical considerations**

A: What is the best seating configuration for the presentation?

F: Whatever configuration you use, the most important consideration is that the students be able to see the speaker well.

Speakers incorporate a lot of body movement in expressing themselves, so it's best if the audience can see them from head to toe. You also want the seats up as close as possible to the speaker—you don't want a big gap between the speaker and the audience. If the assembly is going to take place in the gym, have the entire audience seated on one side if possible. (If the school has an auditorium, that is a far better room for the presentation than the gym.)

A: Many schools have very poor sound systems. Do you suggest speakers invest in their own systems?

F: For speakers who are on the road a lot, bringing your own system is not practical. School sound systems are much better these days. Speakers with special needs often choose to carry their own microphone that can be readily patched into the school's system. Once again, it's important to emphasize to the school that a quality sound system is mandatory. When a speaker has to use a poor sound system, they are absolutely exhausted at the end of the program and the audience is not as attentive. Speakers' voices are their instruments—they have to protect them. If they are constantly projecting their voices in order to be heard, they will destroy their vocal cords.

## PROGRAM DESCRIPTION

### Substance abuse

In elementary schools, speaking is often combined with music or other art forms to convey a message about the dangers of substance abuse in a way that is accessible for young students. Jana Stanfield is a nationally known singer, songwriter, and speaker from Nashville, Tennessee. Each year during *Red Ribbon Week*, a nation-wide calendar designation designed to spotlight drug-abuse prevention efforts, Jana presents a series of programs addressing the issue of alcohol and drug abuse. Combining songs, stories, and speaking, Jana's program, *Wisdom From Unlikely Sources,* provides practical advice that helps students stay clear of substance abuse. In a recent interview, Jana described her program:

> After I begin the program with a song entitled *Wake Up and Dream*, I tell the kids that I am going to give them the three best pieces of advice that I ever learned and that the advice will help them do whatever it is they want to do in life. I tell them that I heard the advice from an unlikely source—a nine-year-old boy—and that I'm going to tell them about the boy later in the program.
>
> The first piece of advice I give them is *stay awake*. We talk about what it means to stay awake—awake to what is going on both outside of you and inside of you. We talk about that inner voice that, if you listen, guides you and tells you what is good for you and what is not good for you. I explain how part of staying awake is keeping the mind alert—not doing anything that takes away from our ability to do the things we want to do with our lives.
>
> Introducing the second piece of advice—*hold on*—I tell them how I grew up in an alcoholic family. I describe what it was like to watch someone I loved ruin their life with alcohol. We talk about the importance of holding on to the people, places, and things that can offer support in times of trouble. Together, the kids and I come up with a list of six different kinds of people we can always count on. At this point, I really try to support the school counselors and other people or programs that are in place at the school to help students. Then I sing *If You'll Just Listen to Me*—a song about talking with others about what is going on inside us.
>
> The third piece of advice is *never give up*. I talk to students about some of the stars I've met in Nashville and some of their struggles—that it wasn't always easy for them. We talk about how important it is to keep trying and never give up hope. Then, after I tell them the story behind the song, I sing *If I Had Only Known*—a song about a person in my life I knew I could always turn to.

In the last portion of the program, I tell them a true story about a boy who becomes trapped in an underground drainage tunnel. After the boy was rescued he explains that a frog in the tunnel gave him the three pieces of advice—*stay awake, hold on,* and *never give up.* During the story, the kids see how this advice helped the boy throughout the ordeal.

Through singing the songs, talking about the personal experiences behind them, and telling the story, I hope to give the students practical tools they can use to stay alcohol and drug free, even in challenging social situations.

# Bibliography and Suggested Reading

*Young Audiences Program Booklet 2: The Performance.* Young Audiences, Inc., 115 East 92nd Street New York, NY 10128

*Young Audiences Program Booklet 1: The Process of Designing.* Young Audiences, Inc., 115 East 92nd Street New York, NY 10128

Roger Parker. *Looking Good in Print.* Ventana Press

James Gibson. *How to Make More in Music.* Workbooks Press

*Designing Arts Education Programs: A Workbook for Artists.* Young Audiences, Inc., 115 East 92nd Street New York, NY 10128

Gerald R. Doan. *Establishing School Programs in Chamber Music.* Free from Chamber Music America, 305 Seventh Avenue, New York, NY 10001-6008

Bertie Synowiec. *Strategies for Marketing Your Program to Schools.* (For speakers.) Positive Support Seminars, 8950 Macomb Street, Suite 2, Grosse Ile, Michigan 48138

Carol Cummings. *Managing to Teach.* Teaching Inc. Edmonds, WA

# Appendix

Organizations that focus on integrating educational activities into music lessons and curriculum:

> Dalcroze Society of America
> c/o Anne Farber
> 161 W. 86th St. No. 7A
> New York, NY 10024
> (212) 724-5009

> Organization of American Kod'aly Educators
> c/o Glenys Wignes
> 1457 S. 23rd St.
> Fargo, ND 58103-3708
> (701) 235-0366

> American Orff-Schulwerk Association
> P O Box 391089
> Cleveland, OH 44139-8089
> (216) 543-5366

A national service association for chamber musicians:

> Chamber Music America
> 305 Seventh Avenue
> New York, NY 10001-6008
> (212) 242-2022

A national organization bringing performing artists into schools:

> Young Audiences, Inc.
> 115 East 92nd Street
> New York, NY 10128
> (212) 831-8110

Dance-education organizations:

> Dance Educators of America
> P O Box 509
> Oceanside, NY 11572
> (516) 766-6615

> Dance Masters of America
> P O Box 610533
> Bayside, NY 11361-0533

Theater-education organizations:

Educational Theater Association
3368 Central Parkway
Cincinnati, OH 45225-2392
(513) 559-1996

Public Speaking organizations:

Gavel Clubs
c/o Daniel Rex
P O Box 9052
Mission Viejo, CA 92690-7052
(714) 858-1207

National Speakers Association
1500 S. Priest Drive
Tempe, AZ 85281
(602) 968-2552

International Platform Association
P O Box 250
Winnetka, IL 60093
(708) 446-4321

Jostens Speakers Bureau
P O Box 727
Danville, CA 94526
1-800-541-4660 / 510-831-1229

Storytelling organizations:

National Story League
c/o Virginia Dare Shope
1342 4th Ave. Juniata
Altoona, PA 16601
(814) 942-3449

National Storytelling Association
P O Box 309
Jonesborough, TN 37659
(423) 753-2171

Puppetry organization:

Puppeteers of America
5 Cricklewood Path
Pasadena, CA 91107
(818) 797-5748

Unicycling, juggling and sports organizations:

Unicycling Society of America
P O Box 40534
Redford, MI 48240
(810) 661-0334

International Jugglers Association
P O Box 218
Montague, MA 01351
(413) 367-2401

International Rope Skipping Organization
P O Box 20053
Boulder, CO 80308-3053
(303) 444-6961

School mail list brokers:

Patterson's Educational Mailing Lists
(847) 459-0605

Educational Mailing Lists Clearing House
(815) 335-6373

List of state arts commissions:

National Association of State Arts Commissions
1010 Vermont Avenue NW, Suite 920
Washington D.C. 20005
(202) 347-6352

Drug-abuse prevention information:

National Clearing House for Alcohol/Drug Information
1-800-729-6686

Federal grant information:

Capitol Publications, Inc.
1-800-221-5597

# Index

# Silcox Publications

**Additional copies of this book** may be ordered at the price of $18.95 plus $2.00 shipping and handling.

**Marketing to schools:** A supplemental publication exploring the topic of marketing to schools is available for $9.95 plus $2.00 shipping and handling. This Special Report contains information on writing effective copy for school promotional materials, samples of several promotional pieces created by Silcox Productions to promote school assembly programs, and a discussion of the pros and cons of various promotional strategies.

**Designing homemade promotional pieces:** Due to be published in 1997, this guidebook provides step-by-step instructions for creating posters, brochures, cover letters, post-cards, letterhead stationary, and other promotional pieces at your kitchen table. Copywriting, design, appropriate use of fonts, enlarging and reducing copy, and many others concepts are covered in detail. Please call for availability and price.

**Quantity discounts** are available to bookstores, catalog houses, schools, universities, arts organizations, etc. Please call for additional information.

**Reprints of individual chapters** are available for educational workshops and seminars. Please call for details.

**Professional consulting** is available at a very reasonable fee. Services include critique and evaluation of existing programs and personal guidance in creating a new program. Please call for details.

Please direct orders and inquiries to:

Silcox Productions
P O Box 1407
Orient WA 99160
(509) 684-8287